LAUGHTER
THE BEST MEDICINE®
HOLIDAYS

LAUGHTER
THE BEST MEDICINE®
HOLIDAYS

HO-HO-HA!
The Merriest Jokes,
Quotes, and Cartoons

Reader's
Digest

The Reader's Digest Association, Inc.
New York, NY/Montreal

A READER'S DIGEST BOOK

Copyright ©2012 The Reader's Digest Association, Inc.
All rights reserved. Unauthorized reproduction, in any manner, is prohibited.
Reader's Digest and Laughter, the Best Medicine are registered trademarks of The
Reader's Digest Association, Inc.

FOR READER'S DIGEST
Project Manager and Art Director: Elizabeth Tunnicliffe
Project Editor: Barbara Booth
Managing Editor: Lorraine Burton
Senior Editor: Katherine Furman
Senior Art Director: George McKeon
Associate Publisher, Trade Publishing: Rosanne McManus
President and Publisher, Trade Publishing: Harold Clarke
Executive Editor, Reader's Digest North America: Courtenay Smith
Chief Content Officer, Reader's Digest North America: Liz Vaccariello
President, Reader's Digest North America: Dan Lagani
President and CEO, Reader's Digest Association, Inc.: Robert E. Guth

Library of Congress Cataloging-in-Publication Data
Laughter, the best medicine : holidays : ho, ho, ha! the merriest jokes, quotes, and cartoons /
the editors of Reader's Digest.
    p. cm.
  ISBN 978-1-60652-546-3 (pbk. : alk. paper) -- ISBN 978-1-60652-548-7 (epub)
  ISBN 978-1-60652-547-0 (adobe)
  1. Christmas--Humor. I. Reader's Digest Association.
  PN6231.C36.L38 2012
  818'.602080334--dc23

                        2012010240

Cover and spot illustrations: George McKeon
Cartoon Credits: Ian Baker: 6; John Caldwell: 64, 120, 159, 172, 177;
Dave Carpenter: 18, 47, 52, 96, 127, 151; Roy Delgado: 15, 30; Joe di Chiarro: 10;
Ralph Hagen: 110, 139, 145, 179, 182; Mike Lynch: 71, 188; Harley Schwadron: 89;
Steve Smeltzer: 59, 74, 83, 104; Thomas Bros.: 37, 101, 115; Kim Warp: 27;
WestMach: 22, 40, 134, 154, 165

We are committed to both the quality of our products and the service we provide
to our customers. We value your comments, so please feel free to contact us.

                The Reader's Digest Association, Inc.
                Adult Trade Publishing
                44 S. Broadway
                White Plains, NY 10601

For more Reader's Digest products and information, visit our website:
                www.rd.com (in the United States)
                www.readersdigest.ca (in Canada)

Printed in China

1 3 5 7 9 10 8 6 4 2

❄ ❄ ❄ ❄ ❄ ❄ ❄ ❄ ❄ ❄ ❄ ❄ ❄ ❄

A Note from the Editors

If you rely on television commercials, you'd think the winter holidays are a time of loving perfection: clean homes, well-behaved children, meticulously wrapped gifts, perfect cuisine, distinguished guests, and perpetual, shiny white smiles.

Then there are the holidays as they actually happen in most households. Visits from strange relatives. Food disasters. Awkward parties with coworkers who ignore you the other 364 days of the year. Tangled strands of lights. Pine needles everywhere. Shopping, cleaning, cooking— repeated in an endless cycle for what feels like months on end. Over-sugared children bouncing off the walls in anticipation. Going to bed at 1:00 a.m., exhausted, yet with so much more to do the next day. Oh, joyous season!

If ever there was a time of year in which we need a sense of humor, it's the holidays in America. We're here to help. The stories, one-liners, cartoons, quotes, and jokes in the pages that follow capture the zaniness of the holiday season in all its glory. What makes these jokes so funny is *recognition,* the sense that we've all been there. And you know what? We wouldn't want it any other way. Because holiday joy isn't found in perfection; it's really right there in the shared madness!

❄❄❄❄❄❄❄❄❄❄❄❄❄❄❄

Contents

Giving Thanks

"One of the great unsolved mysteries of life is how you can get 24 pounds of leftovers from an 18-pound turkey."

—ROBERT ORBEN

"Everyone who disappeared was plump....
I'm just sayin'."

Fowl Humor

Around noon on Thanksgiving Day, I saw our young newlywed neighbors, Pam and Chuck, emerging from their house. They were dressed up, and I assumed that they were on their way to Thanksgiving dinner with one or the other set of parents, both of whom lived in the area. Later that afternoon, I saw them again—dressed in sweat suits as they jogged by with a cheery wave. Still later I heard them exchanging hellos with my husband. They were again dressed up and going somewhere.

The next day, Pam explained: "We didn't want to offend either my parents or Chuck's. They both have big traditional Thanksgiving dinners. So we ate one huge dinner with his family in the afternoon, came home to jog it off, then ate another huge dinner with my family in the evening."

—SONIA E. MASELLO

Last Thanksgiving morning, knowing that my sister had invited some of her husband's relatives to dinner, I dropped in to see how she was coming along. The house was in a shambles, and her four little daughters were squabbling among themselves. When she came out of the kitchen to greet me, her hair was a mess, she had turkey dressing all over her hands, and flour on her face. Before I could say anything, she looked at me and muttered, "Those damn pilgrims!"

—MRS. NED C. CARLSON

While our son was in training at Fort Knox, we joined him for Thanksgiving Day dinner at the base. On leaving the mess hall, we passed the kitchen, and I asked him if they had electric dishwashers. "Sure, Mom," he replied. "We just take a new recruit and plug him in."

—MRS. FRED PFEIFFER

❋ ❋ ❋ ❋ ❋ ❋ ❋ ❋ ❋ ❋ ❋ ❋ ❋ ❋

A three-year-old's report on Thanksgiving: **"I didn't like the turkey, but I liked the bread he ate."**

—ART LINKLETTER

As I was basting the beautiful turkey we were having for Thanksgiving and calculating that we might have enough left over for Sunday dinner, too, my nephew came into the kitchen to watch me.

"How many stoppers are we going to have today?" he asked.

"Stoppers?" I asked. "What do you mean?"

"You know, all those courses you have first, to stop people from eating so much turkey."

—ELSIE CHASE

As the only vegetarian in my family, I often get tired of defending my food choices to other family members, especially at the large dinner gatherings we have on special occasions. I didn't realize how often the subject is actually discussed until one day around Thanksgiving, when I picked up my six-year-old son, Jordan, from school. His class had made Thanksgiving turkey crafts using potatoes and paper feathers.

Jordan proudly presented his to me, announcing excitedly, "Mom, this year we'll finally have the kind of turkey even you can eat!"

—CHARLOTTE REARDON

Many of us Kiowas have married "palefaces," but we remain proud of our Indian heritage. When my cousin invited her out-of-state in-laws for Thanksgiving dinner, a Kiowa relative asked who her guests were.

"Oh," she replied, "the pilgrims came to eat with us today."

—ALLEN C. QUETONE

❄ ❄ ❄ ❄ ❄ ❄ ❄ ❄ ❄ ❄ ❄ ❄ ❄ ❄ ❄

Setting the table for Thanksgiving dinner, our kids weren't sure where to place some of the special dishes. After moving one dish, they noticed that juice from the cranberry sauce had spilled, leaving a large red stain on the tablecloth. "Well," quipped ten-year-old Emily, "at least now we'll know where to put the cranberry sauce next year."

—JULIE EMOND

I worked on a toll road, answering the phone, collecting money, and issuing toll tickets. One Thanksgiving Day a woman called to ask about road conditions on the turnpike. After I said everything was A-OK, she told me a friend was coming for dinner. Then came the stumper: "If my friend just left from exit twelve," she asked, "what time should I put the turkey in?"

—SANDRA SHIELDS

When an English business associate was visiting in our home one Thanksgiving, our young son asked him whether the English celebrated Thanksgiving.

"Oh, yes, indeed," replied our friend. "But we celebrate it on the Fourth of July!"

—DONALD W. DAVIS

The host was carving the turkey and taking requests. "White meat? Dark? Some of both?"
One guest asked, "Is that white good?"
The host looked at him for a moment, then said solemnly, **"Nothing but the breast."**

—JOHN A. CHARTERS

꽃 꽃 꽃 꽃 꽃 꽃 꽃 꽃 꽃 꽃 꽃 꽃 꽃 꽃

Thanksgiving is when one species ceases to gobble and another begins.

—R. E. MARINO

The manager of the cafeteria in a large eastern plant decided that his order of 350 turkeys for Thanksgiving dinner was more than would be needed. He called the purchasing department and asked them to tell the supplier to cut the order in half.

Four days before Thanksgiving, the order was received at the cafeteria loading platform. Sure enough: 350 turkeys, all neatly cut in half.

—ELISE TYNAN

I was amazed, when I returned home from school for Thanksgiving Day, to find a lavishly prepared dinner. You see, my mother is not what one might term a proficient cook. For a woman who, six months before, could have destroyed a can of vegetable soup, the preparation of such a handsome turkey with full trimmings seemed impossible.

Then my father said the blessing, and I understood. "Our Father," he began, "we thank thee for this fine day. We thank thee for our fine son. And most of all, we thank thee for Harry's Delicatessen, which made this dinner possible."

—MICHAEL WALKER

A teacher displayed pictures her second-graders had drawn after hearing about the pilgrims' voyage and the first Thanksgiving. One drawing, by an army child, a veteran of many army moves, caught our attention. There, among the pilgrims, Indians, and turkeys, was a moving van with the name "Mayflower" written on it.

—MRS. H. R. TODD

❋ ❋ ❋ ❋ ❋ ❋ ❋ ❋ ❋ ❋ ❋ ❋ ❋ ❋

The pro football team had just finished practice when a turkey strutted onto the field.

"I want to try out," the turkey told the coach.

Stunned, the players stared as the bird caught pass after pass and ran right through the defensive line.

After 30 minutes the coach had seen enough. "You're excellent," he said. "Sign with us, and you'll get a huge bonus."

"Forget the bonus," the turkey said. "All I want to know is, does the season go past Thanksgiving?"

—UNKNOWN

After years of cooking meals for four strapping sons, I found it hard to adjust to cooking for just myself. One Thanksgiving when the boys couldn't make it home, I decided to have roast turkey anyway.

At the local poultry market, I took my time checking the birds, but they were all too large. Finally I asked the patient clerk if he had anything smaller.

"Indeed we do, ma'am," he said. "We call them eggs."

—JOAN THOMPSON

At a family meeting to decide where to celebrate the holidays, my newest son-in-law turned to my daughter and said, "Well, we have to have Thanksgiving and Christmas with either your mom or your sister."

Touched that he loved his new family so much, I started to hug him as my eyes misted over. Then he added, **"They have satellite dishes!"**

—FRANCES BRADLEY

For our first Thanksgiving, my wife's parents came over
for dinner. My bride roasted a beautiful turkey,
which she brought to the table on a silver tray.
With a very sharp knife, I carved it into lovely piles
of thinly sliced white and dark meat. I smiled at my
father-in-law, a well-known surgeon, and said,
"How was that for a stunning bit of surgery?"
He laughed and replied,

"Not bad.
Now let's see you put it back together."

—CARL ROSS

My sister Donnelly is a whiz in the kitchen, while my other
sister and I are culinary klutzes. So she was understandably
hesitant when Maureen and I insisted on making Thanksgiving
dinner on a visit to her house. After Donnelly left for work on the
day of our big meal, we studied the oven manual, set the timer,
and left to go skiing, feeling quite proud of our accomplishment.

The feeling lasted until six hours later, when we returned—
to a nice hot oven and a raw turkey sitting on the kitchen counter.

—NANCY MARLATT

A friend's college roommate was enjoying Thanksgiving
dinner at home when he accidentally overturned his cup of tea.
Forgetting that he was in the presence of his family, he released a
flood of profanity. His grandmother, visibly shocked, said to him,
"You eat with that mouth?"

—D. D.

"No, I haven't seen the cat since I put the
turkey out to thaw."

Thanksgiving menu: **roast turkey, candied yams, and pickled relatives.**

—ARNOLD H. GLASOW

After Thanksgiving dinner, the adults gathered in the living room to exchange reminiscences, while the children went into the family room to play. Suddenly our hostess noticed that an elderly relative was missing. "Where's Aunt Florence?" she asked. From across the room came a masculine drawl, "Oh, she's with the kids, bridging the generation gap."

—FLORENCE M. MORTIMER

I was stuffing the Thanksgiving turkey when my 2½-year-old son, Joshua, zoomed into the kitchen and saw what I was doing.

With his eyes popping, he came to a quick stop and asked, "Why are you stuffing sandwiches into the turkey's pockets?"

—DEIRDRE CASKENETTE

On Thanksgiving weekend, when my father was recuperating from surgery, his friendly and efficient nurse stopped by. Dad asked her if his doctor would be in to see him that day. "No," she replied, "he's home cooking turkey for his family."

Surprised, Dad asked how she knew so much about his affairs. "I'm his wife," she said.

—CAREN SHUTTLEWORTH

What did the turkey say upon receiving an invitation to Thanksgiving dinner?

"No, thanks. I'm stuffed."

———————————————— JAYNELLE ST. JEAN

❀ ❀ ❀ ❀ ❀ ❀ ❀ ❀ ❀ ❀ ❀ ❀ ❀ ❀ ❀

For 30 years, frantic chefs have called the Butterball Turkey Talk-Line for tips on how to save their Thanksgiving dinner. Here are some of the less appetizing calls.

A disappointed woman phoned in, wondering why her turkey had no breast meat. After a conversation with a Talk-Line operator, it became apparent that the woman's turkey was upside-down.

A gentleman called to tell the operator he cut his turkey in half with a chain saw and wanted to know if the oil from the chain would adversely affect the turkey.

One caller told the operator she had always cut the legs off the turkey before putting it in the oven, thinking that was the method everyone used. She later learned that her mother had been doing that because it was the only way to get the bird in their small oven.

—BUTTERBALL TURKEY TALK-LINE

I was reading a book aloud to my class about Squanto and the first Thanksgiving. Near the end, I came to the part about the great feast where people gathered together, partied, and celebrated for days. I paused to add, "And we all know the name of that special celebration...."
One student called out, "Woodstock!"

—CHRISTINE SWANSON

"QUOTABLE QUOTES

"Thanksgiving is an emotional holiday. People travel thousands of miles to be with people they only see once a year. And then discover once a year is way too often."

—JOHNNY CARSON

"Stress cannot exist in the presence of a pie."

—DAVID MAMET

"Thanksgiving is the one occasion each year when gluttony becomes a patriotic duty."

—MICHAEL DRESSER

"I celebrated Thanksgiving in an old-fashioned way. I invited everyone in my neighborhood to my house, we had an enormous feast, and then I killed them and took their land."

—JON STEWART

"Thanksgiving dinners take eighteen hours to prepare. They are consumed in twelve minutes. Half-times take twelve minutes. This is not coincidence."

—ERMA BOMBECK

"Thanksgiving, man. Not a good day to be my pants."

—KEVIN JAMES

"A lot of Thanksgiving days have been ruined by not carving the turkey in the kitchen."

—KIM HUBBARD

"We're having something a little different this year for Thanksgiving. Instead of a turkey, we're having a swan. You get more stuffing."

—GEORGE CARLIN

"You can tell you ate too much for Thanksgiving when you have to let your bathrobe out."

—JAY LENO

"I asked my mother-in-law to bring a vegetable."

Thanks, I Guess

Before we sat down to our Thanksgiving dinner, my wife spoke of our many blessings. First on her list came our six healthy children. An hour later, when we were at the table, all was pandemonium. Noticing that my wife's eyes were closed, I asked her what was the matter. "Nothing," she said. "I am just praying for patience to endure my blessings."

—E. C. STEVENSON

After sitting down to a grand Thanksgiving spread at my mother-in-law's home, she announced, "Before we get started, I think we ought to give thanks to the Lord." Without skipping a beat, her sister grumbled,

"I think we better taste the meal first."

—STEVE WISE

The oven on my almost-new stove hadn't worked in weeks, and frequent calls to the serviceman produced no results. As Thanksgiving approached, I told my husband that this year we would be having boiled turkey.

"I'll have that oven fixed in time for Thanksgiving," he promised.

The week before the holiday, the serviceman at last arrived. I asked what magic words my spouse had used. "Oh," replied the serviceman, "your husband just said that if the oven wasn't fixed by Thanksgiving, you were inviting yourselves to my house for dinner. My wife didn't like that idea at all."

—MARGARET HILLER

✽ ✽ ✽ ✽ ✽ ✽ ✽ ✽ ✽ ✽ ✽ ✽ ✽ ✽

Some neighbors of my grandparents' gave them a pumpkin pie as a holiday gift. As lovely as the gesture was, it was clear from the first bite that the pie tasted bad. It was so inedible that my grandmother had to throw it away.

Ever gracious and tactful, she still felt obliged to send the neighbors a note. It read, **"Thank you very much for the pumpkin pie. Something like that doesn't last very long in our house."**

—KRISTA ROSE

My uncle, an Anglican archbishop, was presiding over our family's Thanksgiving dinner. My two daughters, eight and five, had been practicing saying a special grace for the occasion. When my uncle asked if one of them would like to recite it, the youngest quickly volunteered. We all bowed our heads and waited expectantly.

"Dear . . ." she began. There was a prolonged silence, then finally a loud stage whisper to her sister. "Psst! What's His name?"

—K. CURTIS

My grandfather always had the knack of saying the right thing. One Thanksgiving we explained to my younger brother the custom of breaking the turkey wishbone. Eager to have his wish come true, little Philip was bitterly disappointed when he saw that he held the small end of the bone, while his grandfather had the larger part.

"That's all right, my boy," said his smiling grandfather. "My wish was that you would get yours."

—LINDAANN LOSCHIAVO

❈ ❈ ❈ ❈ ❈ ❈ ❈ ❈ ❈ ❈ ❈ ❈ ❈ ❈ ❈

Bless, oh Lord, these delectable vittles. **May they add to thy glory and not to our middles.**

—YVONNE WRIGHT

Last Thanksgiving my niece came home with her school project: a beautiful autumnal leaf with the words "I am thankful for my mommy" printed on it.

Her eyes tearing, my sister said, "This means so much to me."

Her daughter nodded. "I wanted to put 'Hannah Montana,' but my teacher wouldn't let me."

—KERRIANNE WOLFE

The checkout clerk at the supermarket was unusually cheerful even though it was near closing time. "You must have picked up a ton of groceries today," a customer said to the checker. "How can you stay so pleasant?"

"We can all count our blessings," the clerk replied. "The hardest part of this job is the turkeys and the watermelons. I just thank God that Thanksgiving doesn't come in July."

—L. PROCTOR

We were visiting our son, his wife, and our three grand-children for Thanksgiving. As is our custom, before the meal, we each said what we were thankful for. Our grandson Jordi, who is 10, was the last to speak.

"I'm thankful for my family," he said, "and that we could all be together today. I'm thankful for this great meal Mom and Dad cooked.

"But most of all, I'm really thankful I'm not that turkey in the middle of the table!"

—MARILYN FANCEY

❋ ❋ ❋ ❋ ❋ ❋ ❋ ❋ ❋ ❋ ❋ ❋ ❋ ❋ ❋

For a Thanksgiving assignment, my cousin's daughter, who is in first grade, was to draw something she was thankful for. When the teacher collected the drawings, she saw that Rachel's paper was blank. When asked why, Rachel replied, "I wanted to draw a picture of God, but He was too big to fit on the page."

—KATHY HAMM

Our nephew brought a guest to our family's festive Thanksgiving dinner, a stylish young woman who sported a sparkling green stud in her lower lip, a gold stud on her tongue, and an assortment of earrings trailing up her ear. She was introduced to 87-year-old Grandma, who beamed at her and said, "Oh, my, you're already decorated for Christmas."

—MARY ANNA BARKER

The sentence in the Thanksgiving edition of my church bulletin intended to say: "Thank you, Lord, for the many miracles we are too blind to see." But in what might have been a classic Freudian slip, the sentence read: "Thank you, Lord, for the many miracles we are too blond to see."

—ANITA DAUGHERTY

Last Thanksgiving at the height of the hunting season, a couple who live in a beautiful woodland area of New York State asked their four-year-old son to say grace before the holiday dinner. Folding his hands and bowing his head, he prayed:

"Dear Lord, please take care of all the deer and let the hunters shoot each other."

—MARY S. KILBURN

Turkey Day Classics

When a music student brought his French horn to my shop for repair, he complained that the instrument "felt stuffy" and he couldn't blow air through it. It's not unusual to find partial blockages in brass instruments if small items get lodged in the tubing, but when I tested the instrument, the horn was completely blocked.

After much probing and prodding, a small tangerine dropped out of the bell. "Oh," said the musician when I handed him the fruit. Seeing the bewildered look on my face, he explained, "My mom used the horn for a cornucopia in a Thanksgiving centerpiece."

—MARK L. MADDEN

At a U.S. Army–base school, I was presenting the story of the first Thanksgiving to my first-grade class. After talking about why the pilgrims were going to America, we got them on the *Mayflower* and were almost to Plymouth Rock.

Then, using the technique of getting children to imagine themselves in the place of others, I asked, "What would you do if you were about to land in a strange country?" There was a brief, contemplative pause. Then one youngster piped up, "Fasten my seat belt."

—EDNA KNIGHTEN

We had spent most of Thanksgiving Day watching football games on television. As we sat down Friday night to a dinner of leftover turkey, yams, and cold stuffing, our college-age son asked, **"What's this, the instant replay?"**

—BETH OPENSHAW

❋ ❋ ❋ ❋ ❋ ❋ ❋ ❋ ❋ ❋ ❋ ❋ ❋ ❋ ❋

"What a wonderful meal!" wrote a German friend after
 spending Thanksgiving at our home last year.
 "I left your house all fed up."

—ESTHER TISSING

A young housewife with two children is struggling to earn
her college degree. Since her final exams are scheduled for
mid-December, she must spend a lot of time studying. But she
also devotes herself as much as possible to her children and
husband. Around Thanksgiving she confided to me, "I asked Jim
not to look under the bed until Christmas. He thinks it's presents,
but it's only dust."

—S. S.

To keep the guests occupied before Thanksgiving dinner, my
aunt popped a Batman video into the VCR. Almost two hours later
everyone was hungry and had had enough of the flick.

"This movie sure is dragging on," my uncle moaned. "Just
how long is it?"

"Dad," his son said, "why do you think they call it *Batman
Forever?*"

—BRANDY HALL

As a skilled carpenter, I have plenty of work. One September
a customer contracted with me to build extra leaves for an antique
table she had just purchased. She stressed that the job had to be
done by Thanksgiving because she was expecting a crowd for
dinner. Other jobs piled up, however, and I neglected her project.

One evening in mid-November, I received this phone
message: "I'm calling to find out if I need to buy a small tablecloth
or a large tablecloth for Thanksgiving dinner. Please call me back."

I started her job the next day.

—MARTIN G. ANTHONY

"It's an invitation to eat out in the cold in November. Sounds like a nut."

❀ ❀ ❀ ❀ ❀ ❀ ❀ ❀ ❀ ❀ ❀ ❀ ❀ ❀ ❀

Thanksgiving is still a big family day in most homes— they get together during half-time.

—LESTER LANIN

Every Thanksgiving we play a Turkey Bowl football game to determine neighborhood bragging rights. One year our team was close to scoring a game-winning touchdown, so we all listened carefully as our quarterback explained a play to us in the huddle. "I'll look over the defense when we come to the line," he said. "If I call out a color, I'll hand the ball off and we'll run left. If I call out a fruit, I'll throw a pass into the end zone."

Wow, we're actually using strategy this year, I thought. How can we lose with such a wise team leader?

When our quarterback came to the line, he looked around, then barked out the signals: "15, 43, 18, orange, hike!"

—DAN DUGAN

The nun who was the principal at my granddaughter's school called an assembly to announce the results of a fund-raising drive. After a prayer of Thanksgiving by the priest, sister arose and announced the gratifying total. Oohs and aahs were heard as the students clapped with enthusiasm.

"Yes, indeed," sister continued, "we could hardly believe it ourselves. Why, Father and I were pinching each other—"

—HAYDEN ROGERS

Having been an air force brat all my life, I'm used to moving unexpectedly to a new post. But even I was a bit shaken when, at college last November, I received a letter from my father bearing an unfamiliar postmark and saying, "Oh, son, did I tell you? Don't come home to Louisiana for Thanksgiving. We've been transferred to Madrid."

—TIMOTHY K. CORMANY

❋ ❋ ❋ ❋ ❋ ❋ ❋ ❋ ❋ ❋ ❋ ❋ ❋ ❋ ❋

Our neighbor ranks in the top 10 on any list of the nation's most dedicated football fans. Every Saturday, Sunday, and holiday he digs in at the line of scrimmage, squarely in front of the TV set, and with unswerving devotion watches every game scheduled, from opening kickoff to final whistle.

On Thanksgiving morning his teenage daughter sat in my kitchen, listening gloomily as our children made eager inquiries about the status of our turkey: "When will it be ready?" "When do we eat?"

Hoping to cheer our young visitor, I asked brightly, "And what time are you having dinner?"

Her unhappy voice seemed to answer for all the football widows and orphans of America. "At half-time," she muttered.

—JAN WASHBURN

My son is ticket-taker, baggage carrier, and all-purpose expert for a small airline in Augusta, Maine. On Thanksgiving he was planning to take the last flight himself home to Boston. When the plane landed in Augusta, he unloaded the luggage of the arriving passengers, handed it out to them, checked in the new passengers, lined them up at the door, put their bags aboard, and escorted them to the plane. Then he closed up the office and climbed into the plane himself.

As he was shutting the door, one man who had been watching the proceedings carefully tapped him on the shoulder. "Look," he said, "if you're flying this thing, I'm getting off."

—MRS. WILLIAM O. NICHOLS

The windows of playwright Marc Connelly's New York apartment offer a perfect view of Macy's Thanksgiving Day parade. Connelly sends formal invitations to come and watch the parade to the children of his friends, with this postscript: "Parents optional."

—LEONARD LYONS

❀ ❀ ❀ ❀ ❀ ❀ ❀ ❀ ❀ ❀ ❀ ❀ ❀ ❀ ❀

The day before Thanksgiving, one of the professors at pharmacy school presented the class with a surprise quiz. In addition to the usual A, B, C, or D answers, the multiple-choice test had options like R, S, T, and U on some questions. After completing the exam, I knew I had done well, for the letters of my answers spelled out: "Eat a lot of turkey."

—LARRY J. SULLIVAN

I was preparing my nursery-school class for Thanksgiving. Many years ago, I told them, the pilgrims survived a difficult voyage, arrived at Plymouth Rock, and met the Indians, who helped them prepare a great feast. The mother of one of my pupils came in the day after our class discussion. Her daughter had reiterated the story of the pilgrims, and the mother asked her what the menu for the first Thanksgiving had included.

The little girl replied, "I'm not sure, but you can ask my teacher—she was there!"

—JANICE SOFRAN

One Sunday I was scheduled to preach twice: first at my small church and then at a larger church, near the city. After finishing the early service, I left for the second. In my haste, and traveling in unfamiliar territory, I got lost. Finally reaching the church, I heard the strains of the opening hymn. I hurried in and took my place next to the pastor.

When the hymn ended, I stood up and gave the prayer of Thanksgiving. After I sat down, my colleague turned to me and said, "Who are you?"

After I told him, he informed me that I was at the wrong church. He then explained my gaffe to the congregation, and I again walked down the aisle, this time to applause.

—RICHARD J. HENDRY

Yuletide
Cheer

"Santa Claus has the right idea.
Visit people once a year."

—VICTOR BORGE

'Tis the Season

We make a lot of fruitcakes, and for special occasions we ice them with marzipan. Just before Christmas my daughter-in-law, Heather, called to ask me for the icing recipe. During our conversation, she mentioned that she'd told some friends about the cakes she was making, and one friend asked her how she learned to make them.

"It was easy!" Heather told her. "I called my mother-in-law. She's the queen of fruitcakes!"

—PAM NORTHCOTT

Last year in August, my wife, Louise, announced that she wanted a new stove because the timer on our 25-year-old model wasn't working. "Why do you need a new stove?" our son Wade asked. "You don't cook."

"I do," she countered. "I cook a turkey at Christmas."

In early September she got a new stove. In October, Wade asked, "When are you going to cook something on it?"

"Is it Christmas already?" she asked.

—DAVID HODGKINSON

The popular and busy men's clothing shop in a neighboring town employed a dedicated staff who always helped clients select just the right items. At Christmas every year, they added a festive touch—a bowl of mixed candies on the counter.

One day, after having made numerous purchases, an older woman leaned over the counter, smiled at the young clerk, and said, "Now, my dear, may I please have a kiss?"

Mindful of good customer relations, the young man leaned over and planted a kiss on the woman's cheek.

"No, no," the customer laughed. "I meant the candy kisses."

—CATHERINE J. BLENKHORN

When my husband and I were newly married, he received his first bonus check—for $15. I was duly impressed and asked what he intended to do with it. "Put it in the bank," he said. I protested that it was a gift and, since it was Christmas, he should get something special with it, something he wanted. "That's what I want," he replied. "Money in the bank."

—MRS. R. C. DARRE

This story is about Jack Straus, chairman of the board of Macy's. One Christmas Eve he returned late to his New York apartment, having worked until midnight ensuring that all Christmas orders were filled in the "world's largest store." He climbed wearily into bed, and at two o'clock in the morning the phone rang. He picked up the receiver.

"Hello, Mr. Jack Straus of Macy's?"

"Yes."

"Oh, Mr. Straus, I was in your store the other day, and I found the most adorable ski hat for my husband. It's in his stocking, and I just can't wait for him to see it."

"May I ask," he replied with chilling politeness, "what prompts you to call me at this hour of the night about a ski hat?"

"Because your darn truck just delivered it," came the shouted reply as the phone was slammed down.

—J. S. Z.

One December morning I headed down the steps to catch my subway, the L train. A sign on the platform declared that the line was not running, but there was bus service aboveground. I was rushing back up the stairs when I passed two women descending. "No L," I gasped as I ran by.

"And a Merry Christmas to you, too," they called out, continuing down the stairs.

—MIKE CAMPBELL

I work in the dress department of a large store, and each Christmas I watch for my favorite customer, a small, dignified elderly gentleman. He carefully examines every dress on the size 16½ rack and, after making his choice, moves to the size 22½ rack, where he selects the identical dress. I gift-wrap the size 16½ and hold the 22½ until the day after Christmas, when his smiling wife comes in to exchange sizes.

—ELAINE HALLIGAN

While packing a box to send to our son for his first Christmas in the air force, I decided to follow an old family custom and add a stocking full of toys and games. When he called home on Christmas Day, I asked nervously if the package had caused him any embarrassment.

"Well," he said, "right now two guys are up on the barracks roof flying the glider plane; there's a bet on who can keep the paddle ball up the longest; the wind-up cars are being raced; everybody's been shot with the water pistol. I haven't even had a chance to play with my own stuff."

—MRS. T. LESNICK

I enjoy dressing up for the holidays, so when my family gathered for dinner at a nice restaurant, I wore a sweater with five little Santas on the front. Each Santa had a real bell sewn onto his hat. When the waiter came to our table, he turned to me, "What a festive sweater. Do they jiggle?"

Red-faced, he corrected himself. **"I mean, jingle."**

—MOLLY D. SLOAN

"I'm pretty sure it was over the river."

We purchased an old home in northern New York State from two elderly sisters. Winter was fast approaching, and I was concerned about the house's lack of insulation. "If they could live here all those years, so can we!" my husband confidently declared.

One November night the temperature plunged to below zero, and we woke up to find interior walls covered with frost. My husband called the sisters to ask how they had kept the house warm. After a brief conversation, he hung up. "For the past thirty years," he muttered, "they've gone to Florida for the winter."

—LINDA DOBSON

Man to man: **"All I expect for Christmas is my wife's relatives."**

—EARL WILSON

Last Christmas my wife, Laura, was counting calories to minimize the inevitable holiday pounds. She asked me to hide her favorite snacks in a cupboard too high for her to reach, even with a chair. When I came home from work that evening, I saw the nearly empty bag of Bugles sitting on the counter.

"How'd you get those down?" I asked, surprised.

"With a little eggnog," Laura sheepishly replied.

—JARRETT SYLVESTRE

To lighten the postmen's load during the Christmas rush, Toronto postal authorities arranged with strategically located residents to leave sacks of mail on their porches. The first day one postman arrived to collect such a sack on his route, he found none there and supposed none had been left. But when it happened again the next day, he reported it to his supervisor.

Mail had been left, so an investigator called on the householder and asked if she hadn't agreed to have the mail left there during the Christmas season.

"I did," said the woman. "And it's the last time, too. I don't mind helping out, but the last bag you left took me two and a half hours to deliver."

—ROSEMARY BREW

Just as I began my Christmas Eve service, the electricity in the church failed. The ushers and I found some candles and placed them around the sanctuary. Then I reentered the pulpit, shuffled my notes, and muttered, "Now, where was I?"

A tired voice called out, "Right near the end!"

—REV. DOUGLAS C. WOODS

It was the Sunday before Christmas, and our young new pastor was sharing with the congregation the somewhat ambitious goal he had set for himself the previous December: to visit every church family in their homes before the year ended. Apologizing for not quite achieving his aim, he asked that anyone desiring a visit before the year's end please raise his hand. We all looked as one person raised her hand. It was the pastor's wife.

—SHARON MACY

The local minister was fond of an occasional tipple, so the owner of a bar offered him a crate of cherry brandy for Christmas in exchange for a free advertisement in the church newsletter.

The minister reluctantly agreed and ran the following message in the next issue: "The pastor would like to thank Patrick O'Reilly for his kind gift of a crate of fruit and for the spirit in which it was given."

—WILLIAM ROSS

As an instructor, I try to lighten the stress of important exams by sticking in a lighthearted question at the end. Before Christmas break one year, the last question read: "Your instructor wishes you: (a) an enjoyable holiday; (b) a happy New Year; (c) a restful vacation; (d) all of the above."

One of my students, correctly anticipating his low grade on the exam, added a choice of his own: "(e) had studied more!"

—LINDA PAYNE

How many reindeer does it take to change a lightbulb?

Eight. One to screw it in, and seven to hold Rudolph in place.

"**S**ome people are squeamish about raising their own holiday turkeys—but not me. Back in January we bought a turkey who became like a member of the family. We kept him in the house, fed him, and took him for walks. But when the time came, there was no nonsense about it. We had him for Christmas dinner. He sat on my right."

—ROBERT ORBEN

I was a vegetarian until I got married. One Christmas, as our children and their families gathered around the table, my husband, Cyril, announced,

"Your mother didn't know what a turkey was until she met me."

—LORRAINE LARKIN

One December, when I was assistant manager of a children's bookstore, we set up a special rack of small holiday books. Looking at a few of the Hanukkah books on display, a customer remarked to the counter clerk how well priced they were.

"Yes," the clerk agreed. "And they make great stocking stuffers, too!"

—KIMBERLY C. PETERSEN

I bought three additional strands of exterior Christmas lights. As my husband and son were busy when I wanted them put up, I decided to do it myself. I climbed up the ladder to the roof, hung over the edge, and secured the wires under the eaves. Back on the ground, with knees still quivering, I flipped the switch and stood back to admire the effect. Seventy-five empty light sockets stared back at me.

—LYNNE BAUMANN

In the midst of the most chaotic traffic, my husband, late and impatient, put his hand full on the horn and left it there, honking away. A woman in the car next to ours leaned over and asked me, "And what else did he get for Christmas?"

—MARIA NATAL CARVALHO

A friend of mine married a fellow named Sherlock. Easy to remember, I thought. I'll just think of Sherlock Holmes. Not long after, however, I sent out my Christmas cards, and my friend called me, laughing.

I had addressed their card to Mr. and Mrs. Holmes.

—SONYA CARSWELL

While Christmas shopping, I asked a pretty college freshman working in our local bookstore during the holiday rush for a copy of Dickens's *Christmas Carol*. Smiling sweetly, she said, "Oh, he didn't write songs. He wrote books."

—ANNABEL COWAN

As a new minister, I wanted my first holiday services to be both attractive and meaningful. The Christmas Eve service included a candle-lighting ceremony in which each congregant lit a candle from his neighbor's candle. At the conclusion of the ceremony, the congregation sat hushed, pondering the beauty of the moment.

I rose to announce a hymn and was taken completely by surprise when laughter broke out in response to my invitation: **"Now that everyone is lit, let's sing 'Joy to the World.'"**

—DAVID PINCKNEY

Shortly before Christmas my niece Carolee took her dog Tippy to the groomer. When she picked Tippy up, they sent her home with a beautiful gingerbread man wrapped in holiday cellophane, tied with a red bow. Once home, Carolee put the cookie on a table.

A few days later she returned from work and saw that half the cookie had been eaten.

When Carolee asked her husband about it, he said, "That was Tippy's? No wonder it tasted like liver."

—EDITH HENRY

My friend Shirley had written her last Christmas card and wearily moved on to writing checks to the phone company, the electric company, and a department store. After the holidays the extent of her pre-Christmas exhaustion became apparent when the bank returned one of her checks with an "incorrect signature" notation. She had signed it "Shirley, Bernie and the girls."

—BETH MCMASTER

Married 37 years, my brother- and sister-in-law, Jake and Fran, were chatting with another couple. Jake admired his friend's ornate gold-and-diamond ring and lamented that all he had was a gold washer, indicating his plain gold wedding band.

The following December a small jeweler's box appeared under the Christmas tree for Jake. When he opened it, he found an expensive gold-and-diamond ring. Thanking Fran for the beautiful gift, he added, "You really shouldn't have spent so much money on me."

"Oh, I didn't," she replied. "I took it out of your top dresser drawer. It's the ring I gave you for our twenty-fifth wedding anniversary."

—V. K. HOEPPNER

Working at the post office during the Christmas rush, I saw these words boldly scrawled across a large package: "Nonperishable, unbreakable—have fun!"

—LOWREY MCNEEL

Attending our church's Christmas program, I noticed that many other men there had full beards. Knowing my wife's aversion to facial hair, I teasingly whispered to her, "How do you think I'd look with a beard and mustache?" She whispered back,

"Lonely."

—ROBERT C. BAPTISTA

Under a cultural-exchange program, my family was host to a rabbi from Russia at Christmastime. We decided to introduce him to a culinary treat that was probably not available in his country: We took him to our favorite Chinese restaurant.

Throughout the meal, the rabbi spoke excitedly about the wonders of our country in comparison to the bleak conditions in his homeland. When we'd finished eating, the waiter brought the check and presented each of us with a small brass Christmas tree ornament as a seasonal gift. We all laughed when my father pointed out that the ornaments were stamped "Made in India."

But the laughter subsided when we saw that the rabbi was quietly crying. Concerned, my father asked him if he was offended because he'd been given a gift for a Christian holiday. He smiled, shook his head, and said, "*Nyet.* I was shedding tears of joy to be in a wonderful country in which a Buddhist gives a Jew a Christmas gift made by a Hindu!"

—ALAN ABRAMSKY

"It was just gonna be too difficult to untangle."

As Canadians living in Miami, we often drove back to Canada for vacations. One year we decided to drive up for the Christmas holidays. When we reached the border, the customs official took one look at our Florida license plates and said, "Anyone dumb enough to leave Florida this time of year can't be smart enough to smuggle anything. Go on through!"

—MRS. M. T. SMITH

Every Christmas, composer Giacomo Puccini would send a coffee cake to each of his friends. One year, after he had given his baker the list, which included the name of Arturo Toscanini, he and the conductor had one of their frequent quarrels. It was too late to recall the cake, but Puccini wanted Toscanini to know how he felt. So he sent him a telegram saying: "Cake sent by mistake."

The conductor replied: "Cake eaten by mistake."

—E. E. EDGAR

We were expecting holiday guests, and I was eager to make our house as festive as possible. Every time I came back from the mall, the miniature Dickens-era village under our Christmas tree grew.

I added a train station, chocolate shop, toy store, and bakery. Then I enhanced the cultural life of the village with a school and a gazebo for band concerts.

After one especially productive shopping trip, I put in a restaurant, where the imaginary villagers could have Sunday brunch after attending services at the new church. I happily rearranged the newest pieces and said to my husband, "Do you know what this village really needs?"

"Yes, I do," he answered crisply. "It needs a board of trustees to enact zoning laws to contain expansion."

—JANET PRZYBORSKI

Hoping to make some money on sales commissions, I took a job as a telemarketer. With a prepared script and a list of 300 names, I started my calls.

"Congratulations," I'd say. "You've just won a Christmas ham."

For four hours, as soon as I got the opening pitch out of my mouth, the prospects hung up. Meanwhile, the other telemarketers were making sales right and left. When my supervisor came by to check on my progress, I asked what I was doing wrong.

"Perhaps it's the list," he said, handing me another one. "You've been calling the members of Temple Israel."

—LARRY SOLOMON

Rich, my husband, and I had a hectic holiday schedule encompassing careers, teenagers, shopping, and all the required doings of the season. Running out of time, I got the stationer to print our signature on our Christmas cards instead of signing each one individually.

Soon we started getting cards from friends signed: "The Modest Morrisons," "The Clever Clarks," "The Successful Smiths."

Then it hit me. I had mailed out a hundred cards neatly imprinted "Happy Holidays from the Rich Armstrongs."

—PATRICIA MEES ARMSTRONG

My creative mother enjoys doing crafts, such as making potpourri boxes decorated with ribbon and lace. Sometimes she gets so involved she disappears into her upstairs workroom for hours, forgetting about more mundane things—like making dinner.

One evening I arrived home to find the kitchen empty again. But this time I found a note: "Warning! Small craft advisory: Buy yourself a pizza."

—JANICE DECOSTE

Asked what she was going to do while her two small sons were visiting their grandmother during the Christmas holidays, one mother replied, **"Something I haven't done in years—listen to the silence."**

—CHRISTINE SMITH

Two weeks before Christmas my mother was searching for a Precious Moments ornament. After what seemed like hours, we found a Hallmark store. Mom approached the sales clerk, who looked more like a linebacker than a cashier, and asked if they had any Precious Moments. "Aren't we having one now?" he replied.

—KAREN HOLTZ

After their wedding on December 23, a Galena, Kansas, couple went directly to the farm where they would live instead of taking a honeymoon trip. There on the farm gate they put a huge red ribbon and a sign: "Do not open until December 25."

—A. M. HEISTAND

It was Christmas Day, and we had all gathered for the holiday meal at the home of my husband's parents. After dessert my mother-in-law left the table and returned carrying a bowl filled with slips of paper. Each adult was instructed to take one. Excited, we did so, wondering what surprise she had thought up for us.

My slip of paper instructed me to dry the dishes; another person was told to wash them. Others had to do pots and pans. Then, with all the parents out of the way, Grandma and Grandpa went into the living room and enjoyed their grandchildren.

—MERNA ALEXANDER

Winters have been hard in our part of Ohio, and my husband's spent many an hour shoveling out our long driveway. He often admired our neighbor's snow blower, so one fall day I decided this would make a perfect Christmas gift. I bought one and hid it away for the holidays.

When snow was predicted for December 15, I broke down and gave my husband his present early. He was thrilled. That night, he made sure his new machine was fueled and ready to run. Then he carefully laid out his thermal clothes in preparation for the next day's adventure. He was so excited, he slept fitfully all night.

In the morning, my eager husband dressed quickly and glanced out the window on his way to the door. Sure enough, the ground was covered with a blanket of snow—but not one inch in the driveway. It had been cleared by our neighbor doing us a favor.

—KIM TERLECKY

Two months after Christmas, our post office had finally recovered from the rush of cards, letters, and packages. I was working at the canceling machine when I noticed that a collection of card-size envelopes had been dropped through the mailing slot.

"Could these be Christmas cards in February?" I thought to myself as I reached for the stack. As I shuffled through the envelopes, my suspicion was confirmed, for on the back of each card was handwritten: "Don't ever trust your husband to do anything."

—REG ALEXANDER

When my mother began teaching, she was known as Miss Smeed to her grade 1 students—or so she thought. She found out differently when she met one of the dads the following January.

"I'm so glad to meet you," he said warmly. "Do you know it was Christmas before I found out your name wasn't Mincemeat?"

—NOREEN AULD

"This one can't promise us the video game.
What's your Santa say?"

The nice thing about a gift of money for Christmas is that it's so easily exchanged.

—ARNOLD H. GLASOW

My mother always resists our attempts to simplify her life with modern conveniences. She claims it's more relaxing to wash dishes by hand and just as easy to use a knife as a food processor. Last Christmas, however, we surprised her with a microwave oven.

"Look, Mom," I said, "these brownies took only four minutes to bake. Isn't a microwave marvelous?"

"Just what I need," she retorted. "A machine to make me fat faster!"

—CARRIE S. BROWN

While driving in New York City one evening during the pre-Christmas rush, I was startled when a police officer blew his whistle and motioned me to stop. I certainly couldn't be speeding! I was relieved when the officer, pointing first to my darkened headlights and then to the brilliant Christmas lights and decorations, said, "Madam, won't you help us illuminate Fifth Avenue?"

—DOROTHY L. BONNER

When my wife returned from a shopping trip, she complained that she was having trouble finding the items on my Christmas list. She began naming them: a hydraulic jack, a lug-all hoist, a circular saw, a green toolbox, and a power drill. Baffled, I asked to see the Christmas list. I am a city policeman, not mechanically inclined, and live in an apartment. The problem, I discovered, was that my wife had taken a page from my police notebook—a list of the items in a recent burglary.

—JAMES WEISS

Our department store assigned all new staff a three-digit code so "Wages" knew what rate to pay. One November we recruited a Santa for our grotto. I asked my manager what his code would be.

"0, 0, 0," he replied.

—CURTIS

Two desperate days before Christmas, I was buying gift wrap when I saw a crumpled piece of paper on the counter. It was a Christmas list—almost a twin of the one I was clutching—crossed out, scribbled over, and packed with question marks.

My heart went out to the harried list maker as I read: "Harry—bourbon? Paperweight? Get embroidery hoop and gold paint for Judy's halo. New bills from the bank for mailman. Order pies today." But the last notation was the real heart-wrencher. In big print, it read: "Don't lose list!"

—BEE HARGROVE

When the bishop of Chester, England, declared that there should be a religious message on Christmas stamps, *Punch* magazine suggested, "Lord, deliver us."

—KENNETH THOMAS

One week before Christmas last year, Connecticut was hit by a storm that gained the honor of being the worst ice storm in memory. Over a quarter of a million households were without electrical power or heat. In many houses there was no water. Freezing temperatures drove families to emergency shelters. In some areas five or six days passed before the lights came on. When we returned home six days later, there was one holiday greeting card waiting in the mailbox. It read: No lights, no heat, Noel.

—MARIA C. JOHNSON

Have you noticed how all the new toys need batteries? Years ago, your biggest problem on a cold Christmas morning was getting the car started. Now it's getting the toys started.

—ROBERT ORBEN

Dad doesn't waste words when he writes a letter. One he sent to me at Simmons College was enclosed with airfare home for Christmas vacation.

The letter read: "Dear Sue, here's some bread so you can get back to the breadbox."

—SUSAN MINOR

The ecumenical spirit of goodwill to all men was never brought to my attention more vividly than on a brisk December day in New Haven, Connecticut. As I pressed through the crowds of holiday shoppers, I chanced to hear a warm-hearted matron taking leave of her friend.

"So," she said, "if I don't see you before Hanukkah—have a merry Christmas!"

—WILLIAM FRANCIS

Having reached the far side of 40, my tastes have become somewhat conservative. So when my teenage daughter presented me with an above-the-knee bright-yellow shift as a Christmas gift, I was a bit stunned. I told her the dress was pretty, but added, "This is the kind of dress a woman wears to attract a man, and I already have my man."

With a sidelong glance at her father, she said, **"Well, attract him."**

—JANE A. PENSON

A choir was singing Christmas carols at a shopping center, and at the entrance a sign read: **"Park, the herald angels sing."**

—ANGIE PAPADAKIS

I was in line at the post office early in December. The man in front of me had a package that he was mailing to his sister in Brazil. After weighing the package, the clerk handed him a mailing form and said the postage would be $6.36. The man looked at the package, then at the form. He hesitated a moment.

"Have you a knife?" he asked. The clerk handed him one. The man slit open the package and unwrapped a delicious-looking fruitcake. After cutting the cake into pieces, he pushed it toward the postal employees and said, "The cake isn't worth that much. Merry Christmas!"

—JUNE BROCK

We spent an enjoyable Christmas holiday in New York City, but battling the crowds became too much one day, and we sought refuge in a quiet museum, where I sat writing postcards. It was surely weariness that moved me to add on one card: "New Yorkers are rude people." And it was weariness that caused me to leave the cards, ready for mailing, on a bench.

When we returned home, my family showed me a card that, in addition to my message, said: "Mailed by a rude New Yorker."

—LINDA PRAGER

I was sitting on a bench outside the post office licking stamps for our Christmas cards when I noticed a lad about nine on a nearby bench doing the same job. But this enterprising youth had recruited a helper. He was rubbing the stamps across the waiting tongue of his obedient Saint Bernard.

—W. R. SHIRLEY

My wife of six months and I spent a long time selecting the card we would send to friends on our first Christmas together. We chose a card with a distinctive abstract design and a meaningful message and proudly mailed early. Shortly after the holiday, we received a silver baby rattle from a generous, elderly aunt who apparently misunderstood the message: "A child is born and peace descends."

—DOUGLAS E. LAM

Our daughter, Cindy, who remained in California after graduating from college, has developed an acute sense of things distinctly southern Californian and occasionally sends them back to us in Ohio.

One Christmas she sent gifts in colorful wrapping paper that showed angels with harps on a background of blue sky and billowing clouds. It was traditional holiday wrapping in every respect—except for one thing: All the angels wore sunglasses.

—LEONARD F. WAITE

In preparation for a Christmas Eve performance, some of the members of our church were rehearsing a group of carols. All went well except for one song, which sounded slightly off. After listening carefully, I finally located the source of trouble. One girl, who came from the Deep South, had been singing: "O lil' ol' town of Bethlehem . . ."

—TENA MOHAUPT

Why was the little pointy-eared guy down in the dumps?

He had low elf-esteem.

On Christmas morning my sister opened a large box from her husband. Inside she found a card that said: "Merry Christmas and Happy New Year." Under a second wrapper was a card: "Be my valentine." More paper and strings came off to reveal "Happy Easter," "Happy Birthday" and Mother's Day greetings.

Finally she worked her way through "Happy Wedding Anniversary" to the gift, a beautiful mink stole, and the final card, which read: "Gal, you've had it for this year."

—J. V. RHODES

Excited over the success I'd had with my new diet, I optimistically projected several months into the future and announced to my husband that I was giving him a 110-pound wife for Christmas.

"Oh, good," he answered. "Whose?"

—MARY A. JOHNSON

To show our admiration for his imaginative and interesting lectures, we bought the professor a box of his favorite cigars for Christmas. On the last day of class, the present was on his desk, but much to our surprise he didn't seem pleased. In fact, he acted somewhat annoyed when he unwrapped the box. He said nothing about it, however, until the end of the period.

"Gentlemen," he announced, "the university strictly forbids faculty members accepting gifts from the students. I appreciate your sentiments, but we must obey the rules."

He took the box of cigars and tucked it under his arm. "There is only one course open to me. I shall take them home and burn them."

—BRUCE BROWN

"Don't worry. It's very common for fruitcakes to have self-esteem issues around the holidays."

Like most families, we exchange Christmas cards with some people who are quite unremembered acquaintances. Once on our list, the names seem to stay. The fact that we were no more remembered than they were was evident the year we sent out cards showing a busy family engaged in holiday activities. Printed on them was: "Greetings from the harried Parkers."

To our surprise, we received in return a number of cards addressed to Mr. and Mrs. Harried Parker.

—PATRICIA L. PARKER

Greetings of the season were expressed in a special way by the officers of a Detroit police station. A double sign in front of the station stated on the side facing the suburbs: "Christmas greetings from your police officers." On the side facing the inner city, the sign read: "Christmas greetings from the fuzz."

—MRS. PIERRE PALMENTIER

Posted notice: "Give something warm and fluffy for Christmas. Five groovy puppies."

—ROBERTSON F. SMITH

As the number of sons of our friends Dick and Marge Hitt increased, their Christmas cards carried the signature: "Dick and Marge and the 3 Hitts" or "4 Hitts" or "5 Hitts," depending on the current score. Finally a long-awaited baby girl arrived, and the signature changed to: **"Dick and Marge, 5 Hitts and a miss."**

—MRS. L. R. TJENSVOLD

The Christmas season is really over when you finally get the pins out of your new shirt.

—JACK HERBERT

Facing possible dismissal from West Point because of our low scholastic standing, my roommates and I were forced to spend our Christmas leave at the academy studying for re-exams. We decided it might be appropriate to send the dean of the academic department, Brig. Gen. Harris Jones, a Christmas card. Using the numbers representing our class standings, we signed the card: "#470, #492, #517, class of 1955."

After mailing it, we began to have misgivings. But a few days later a card arrived addressed to the three of us, reading: "Merry Christmas and Happy New Year, from #1, class of 1917."

—J. W. NAPIER

Red's Rite Spot, a diner on the University of Michigan campus, was gay with Christmas decorations. When Red had served a pretty blond coed sitting at the counter, he leaned over and gave her a big smack on the cheek. Before she could protest, he pointed to a twig of mistletoe hanging above her. The mistletoe was attached to a convenient pulley system that ran the length of the counter.

—PAUL CAMPBELL

During the Christmas season, I walked along Chicago's state street with a friend who is a minister. We stopped to look in a store window that displayed a choir of buxom angels dressed in filmy gowns. My friend gazed into the window for a long time. Then he sighed and said, "Oh, my. If they look like that, we're going to have trouble up there, too."

—G. EUGENIE MAFFIOLI

One Christmas card I received was a snapshot of a relative all bundled up in a bathrobe, with a towel around his neck and clutching a hot-water bottle as he soaked his feet. It was inscribed: "No well."

—R. J. KAPSCH

A weary middle-aged woman on a Philadelphia subway during the Christmas rush was struggling to hang on to a strap as well as an armload of packages. She was standing in front of three men who were occupying space for four, and no one made any effort to move. Suddenly a big, burly fellow pushed her aside, thrust his ample posterior into the narrow space, and wiggled in. Then he rose to his feet.

"Merry Christmas," he said as he gallantly offered her the newly won seat.

—NORMAN A. TAYLOR

Grandfather had always been a problem at Christmas— nothing seemed to please him. This year the children and I decided to chip in and give him a $50 bill to spend as he wished. We watched expectantly as Grandfather opened the envelope. He studied the crisp new bill for a moment and then growled, "Humph! General Grant! Worst president we ever had."

—HOWARD W. LUNDGREN

A cartoonist and I, both attached to a special-service unit, teamed up to print Christmas cards, which we sold for 10 cents apiece to our fellow enlisted men and for 25 cents to officers. We were doing a flourishing business, when the officers learned of the price difference. I was called in by our captain to explain.

"There is a 15-cent sir-charge," I announced.

—I. GOLDSTEIN

A young medical student we know received a very expensive microscope from his parents for Christmas. The card was signed: "Mama and Pauper."

—VERREE WAYNE

When an Iowa girl attending college in Alabama was unhappy because she couldn't afford to return home for the Christmas holidays, her many southern friends presented her with a round-trip ticket accompanied by a large handmade card inscribed: "Yankee, go home!"

—MRS. BEN M. HERR

Could I get my husband to address Christmas cards? I wondered. The family was coming. There were shopping, gifts, the tree, cooking and cleaning *ad infinitum*. I arranged cards, stamps, and address book on the table, then hopefully pulled up a chair and said, "Come on, dear. Let's get these out of the way."

He glanced at the array on the table, turned away, and went into his den, while I looked daggers at his back. I heard a drawer jerked open, banged shut. He returned with a high stack of cards, stamped, sealed, and addressed.

"They're last year's," he said. "I forgot to mail them. Now let's go out to dinner and relax—you've been working too hard."

—MARGARET RICE

When our no-particular-breed dog presented us with eight puppies in November, we knew we would be hard put to find homes for all of them. So we enclosed with our Christmas cards this gift certificate: "Redeemable for one puppy after weaning. Accept this gift in the spirit in which it is given—pure desperation." All the puppies got a good home.

—IRA KELSO

"Help me with this. How did the Wakemans get off our card list but stay on our re-gift list?"

Sign in hospital bacteriology lab: **"The staph wishes you a merry Christmas."**

—MRS. DAVE MADDUX

Shortly before Christmas a Texan dropped in at an exclusive New York art gallery and bought three Van Goghs, five Picassos, six Lautrecs, and an assortment of Monets, Manets, and Corots. "There, my dear," he said to his wife. "That takes care of the Christmas cards. Now let's get on with the shopping."

—LEONARD LYONS

During the Christmas season, when I went to the clinic for a checkup, there was an air of gay excitement as doctors and nurses, carrying beribboned packages, hurried by me toward a certain room. Finally my curiosity got the better of me, and I asked my nurse if there was something special going on.

"No," she explained, laughing. "It's just that when anyone on the staff gets a 'Do not open until Christmas' present, they bring it down here to the fluoroscope machine so they can see what's in it."

—RITA R. IRWIN

One hectic afternoon shortly before Christmas, a harried young mother came to my window at the post office with an energetic small boy in tow. While she purchased a large number of stamps, the mischievous youngster ran helter-skelter through the lobby. A little later I glanced across the lobby and saw that the mother had found a way to keep the boy quiet. He was perched on a writing desk, his tongue sticking out. The mother was methodically tearing off stamps, one by one, moistening them on the handy tongue, then applying them to the Christmas cards in her pile.

—LORRAINE B. HERR

The traditional English folk song "The Twelve Days of Christmas" was revised for a school Christmas program in Donna, Texas. The gift list: twelve fields of cotton, eleven owls a-hooting, ten deer a-running, nine jacks a-jumping, eight bonnets-blue, seven doves a-mourning, six armadillos, five oil wells, four prickly pears, three ruby reds, two Brahman bulls, and a mockingbird in a magnolia tree.

—J. BAILEY

We were studying the Book of Proverbs in our Bible study class, and our minister had included the proverb "Better to live on a corner of the roof than share a house with a quarrelsome wife."

There were a few grins and nudges among the husbands, which turned to laughter when my friend, Terri, turned to her husband and said, "While you're up on that roof, take down the Christmas lights."

—KATHY GALE

One Christmas I visited a friend who has eight children. As we picked our way through the cluttered living room, he said, "To many people, certain sounds are symbolic of Christmas—the tinkle of bells, carol singing, the shouts of happy children. To me it's the unceasing crunch, crunch, crunch of plastic toys."

—J. H. BARNES

We had been out of town for the Christmas holidays, and when we returned, we found in our mailbox a note from friends, saying, "We left you a gift in your milk chute." Eagerly we went to the milk chute—and there found a note from our milkman, thanking us for the good bottle of scotch.

—A. M.

The Christmas card we found on the front seat of our car a couple of weeks before Christmas was from the boys at the garage where we park nightly. We were pleased that they should remember us with a greeting. A week later we found another card from them. It read: **"Merry Christmas. Second notice."**

—VIRGINIA ANGEL

During the usual confusion on Christmas Day, I was putting away the dishes when my son rushed up to me and held out a glass of water and a pill. In a voice of authority he said, "Here, take this!"

Without thinking, I swallowed the pill and then, feeling quite foolish, asked what it was.

"A tranquilizer," he replied. "Now come into the living room and see what your grandson and his toy truck have done to your favorite table."

—MRS. ROBERT SCHAEFER

Why is it that nothing makes you feel more wicked than disobeying a "Do not open until Christmas" seal, and that you're always sorry afterward?

—KATHARINE BRUSH

Bride-to-be to friend: "It was Christmas when I first realized that Tom was getting serious. He gave me an electric blanket with dual controls."

—MAGDALENE WIEL

Doing last-minute Christmas shopping, I was loaded down with bulky packages and heading for my car parked several blocks away. I noticed that a car seemed to be following me, and sure enough the driver offered me a lift. As I climbed in, I thanked him.

"Oh, don't thank me," he said with a sigh. "With all that stuff you've got there, I was sure you must be heading for your car—and I've been looking for a parking place for the last thirty minutes."

—TED F. LANGE

A young friend of mine, wondering what to buy his fiancee for Christmas, heard via the grapevine that she longed for a white negligee. This presented a problem, for he was too shy to shop in the lingerie departments for such a garment. But he found a solution. He telephoned several shops and finally heard about a garment that sounded both glamorous and within his price range.

"Would it be possible for you to put it on one of the mannequins in the window?" he asked. The startled salesgirl agreed that it would be. Half an hour later the young man strolled past the shop window. He eyed the filmy creation furtively, turned, and strolled past once more. Then he hastened to the nearest telephone and rang the salesgirl. "I'll take it," he said. "Please have it gift wrapped, and I'll stop in to pick it up at noon."

—ARTHUR J. ROTH

My Christmas cards from A to G have long and chatty notes from me. My lines get briefer by and by; all T to Z receive is "Hi!"

—ELINOR K. ROSE

QUOTABLE QUOTES

"Christmas is the season when people run out of money before they run out of friends."

—LARRY WILDE

"Marry an orphan: You'll never have to spend boring holidays with the in-laws."

—GEORGE CARLIN

"Most Texans think Hanukkah is some sort of duck call."

—RICHARD LEWIS

"I wrapped my Christmas presents early this year, but I used the wrong paper. See, the paper I used said 'Happy Birthday' on it. I didn't want to waste it so I just wrote 'Jesus' on it."

—DEMETRI MARTIN

"A lovely thing about Christmas is that it's compulsory, like a thunderstorm, and we all go through it together."

—GARRISON KEILLOR

"Christmas is a time when kids tell Santa what they want and adults pay for it. Deficits are when adults tell the government what they want— and their kids pay for it."

—RICHARD D. LAMM

"The one thing women don't want to find in their stockings on Christmas morning is their husband."

—JOAN RIVERS

"One of the most glorious messes in the world is the mess created in the living room on Christmas Day. Don't clean it up too quickly."

—ANDY ROONEY

The Big Man

My nine-year-old son, Roman, had received the latest video game console from Santa Claus, but found several months later that he couldn't load any games into it.

Recalling that a warranty had come with the console, I told him, "I have the receipt, so we can take it back to the store."

Roman gave me a puzzled look. Then his eyes widened and he exclaimed, "Santa gives receipts?"

—SUE PENNINO

Christmas was fast approaching when my friend Dawn reminded her eight-year-old son, Ken, that he would soon be visiting with Santa Claus. He seemed unusually resistant to the idea.

"You do believe in Santa, don't you?" Dawn finally asked her son.

He thought hard, then said, "Yes, but I think this is the last year."

—PENNY HARRISON GILL

Our son and his wife took their two children to the store to see Santa Claus. However, when it was time for three-year-old MaKenna to go up and talk to Santa, she became shy and wouldn't go.

Several times, Santa asked her to come to him, but she refused.

Finally, he asked, "Would you like a present?"

"Yes," MaKenna replied.

"Can you come get it?" Santa asked.

MaKenna thought about this for a moment, then said, "Can you throw it?"

—MAE SIBA

"And remember, no texting while driving!"

While in the car, my three-and-a-half-year-old son, Nick, asked me, "Mommy, how does Santa Claus get into all the houses?"

"He goes down the chimney," I answered.

"But we don't have a chimney," he said in a worried voice.

"Oh," I replied, "if there's no chimney, he goes through the front door."

"But what if it's locked?" he persisted.

Thinking fast, I explained, "Yes, that could be a problem, but happily, Santa made a magic key that opens all the doors of all the houses in the world."

He brightened at once. "Oh, like in the song: 'Glory to the new door key'!"

—ALICIA EAKINS

As part of his job as a driver for a florist's shop, my husband, Michael, would dress as Santa for the holiday season. He was a great hit when making flower deliveries.

Once, Michael popped into a drugstore for a last-minute purchase of his own and was asked by the clerk if he had air miles.

"What do I need air miles for?" he laughed. "My reindeer are parked on the roof."

—SUSAN THORN

As we were putting out cookies for Santa on Christmas Eve, I accidentally dropped one. "No problem," I said, picking it up and dusting it off before placing it back on the plate.

"You can't do that," argued my four-year-old.

"Don't worry. Santa will never know."

He shot me a look. "So he knows if I've been bad or good, but he doesn't know the cookie fell on the floor?"

—KELLY LEDOUX

I love playing Santa at the mall. But parents often have trouble getting young children to sit on my knee. It took a lot of coaxing for one little girl to perch there, so I got straight to the point. "What do you want most of all for Christmas?" I asked.

She answered, "Down!"

—MORLEY LESSARD

My nine-year-old son, Gabriel, had heard some rumors at school that Santa wasn't real. He approached me with a big question: "Dad, tell me the truth. Is Santa real?"

I decided to tell him it was us who had bought his latest Nintendo Wii game.

"Really?" he said. "You should have let Santa bring it. That way, it would have been free."

—MARIO RODRIGUEZ

I became aware of the changing times when I asked my six-year-old granddaughter whether she had written her letter to Santa Claus yet. She gave me a rather puzzled look and then said: "No, Gran. I e-mailed him."

—JANE MINAKER

My four-year-old daughter knows that Santa Claus brings presents to children on Christmas Eve. One day, when we were going into a shop, she asked me for a gift, to which I replied that I couldn't because I had to start saving money for Christmas presents. Confused, she asked:

"Why? Do you have to pay Santa Claus?"

—CLARA RIBEIRO

"You see me when I'm sleeping and know when I'm awake? Wow, Santa. Get a life."

Our daughter announced that she no longer believed in Santa Claus and flatly refused to leave milk and cookies out for him on Christmas Eve. Upset at losing a four-year tradition, her father tried bribing and cajoling her. Nothing worked.

Later that evening, to my surprise, she walked into the living room carrying a bowl of oatmeal. Her father helped her put the bowl under the tree, next to eight others just like it. "What on earth are you doing?" I asked. "I thought she didn't believe in Santa."

"She doesn't," he said, beaming. "But the reindeer—they're a different story!"

—KAREN DWYER

I overheard my seven-year-old son and his friends discussing the Tooth Fairy, Easter Bunny, and Santa Claus.

"Steven says it's the parents who bring the toys," he said skeptically, "but I know my parents wouldn't know how to drive the reindeer."

—SHARON PRICE

Kelsey, my seven-year-old daughter, surprised me when she said she couldn't wait for her first confession so she could wipe her soul clean.

"Then," she added, "there's no way I can be on Santa's naughty list!"

—MELISSA HARVEY-DANIELL

What does a teacher call Santa's little helpers?

Subordinate Clauses

My husband took our two sons, six-year-old Devin and four-year-old Chase, to a party where Santa would be handing out gifts. The instructions from the organizers were to bring our own gifts, so I brought beach towels with the kids' names printed on them.

Upon arriving, Devin said he couldn't believe the skinny Santa was actually Santa. His doubt turned to belief when he opened his gift.

"He has to be the real Santa!" he said. "How else would he know my name?"

—PAULETTE RYAN

Both male and female reindeers grow antlers in summer, but males drop theirs at the beginning of winter. Females retain their antlers until after they give birth in spring.

This means that all of Santa's reindeer are females. We should have known that only women would be able to drag a fat man in a red velvet suit around the world in one night without getting lost.

—GRAHAM CAHILL

While working as a mall Santa, I had many children ask for electric trains.

"If you get a train," I would tell each one, "you know your dad is going to want to play with it, too. Is that okay?"

The usual answer was a quick yes. But after I asked one boy this question, he became very quiet. Trying to move the conversation along, I asked what else he would like Santa to bring him.

He promptly replied, **"Another train."**

—GEORGE T. FAURE

Youngster singing about Santa Claus:
"He's making a list—and checking his wife."

—LIDA YARBROUGH

It was the first year that our son, Adair, was old enough to tell Santa what he wanted for Christmas. Before we left for the mall, we asked him what he would ask Santa for, and he confidently replied, "A drum!"

Perched on Santa's knee, Adair was asked what he wanted, and he quietly said, "A drum." Santa then asked what else he wanted.

Unprepared for this opportunity, Adair looked uncertain, then enthusiastically replied, "French fries!"

—JANE-ANN DALE-HUNTER

When my husband, Bill, was stationed in Germany, our four-year-old son, Darren, would often help me think of gifts to send him. So on learning that Bill would be coming home in late fall, I told Darren we should have a Christmas surprise waiting for him.

But I was taken aback by the gift Darren requested for his father from the mall's Santa Claus. "Please, Santa," he asked, "bring me a little brother so we'll have a surprise for Daddy when he comes home."

—JUNE B. SCHUH

I was in the post office just before Christmas, where the wait in line seemed too much for an energetic boy named Josh. He was causing a commotion. Needing to make a call, I took out my cell phone.

When Josh looked at me, his mother said, "Look, she's calling Santa." Josh stood silently by his mom for the rest of the wait.

—VICKI BROWN

To: Santa. Re: Where Are My Gifts?!

If you fear that letter to Santa won't get to the North Pole in time, try e-mailing him. EmailSanta.com sees more than a million missives every year, and each one gets a response, including these:

- I'm sorry, but I don't have a chimney.... I'll leave the cat flap unlocked for you, but please watch out for the litter box! *Jon, 4*

- Mommy and Daddy say I have not been very good these past few days. How bad can I be before I lose my presents? *Christian, 7*

- Did you really run over my grandma? *MacKenzie, 11*

- I'm sorry for putting all that Ex-Lax in your milk last year, but I wasn't sure if you were real. My dad was really mad. *Bri, 7*

- You really don't need to send me the motor home. I know that you won't be able to fit it in your sleigh. I know that the elves won't be able to reach the pedals, and anyway, my mom said I can't get my driver's license yet. *Kyle, 5*

- Pleease! Don't bring me any new clothes. *Kayla, 9*

- Thank you for the remote-control car last year, even though it broke the day after. I know you tried, and that's what counts. *Alex, 8*

- Do you know Jesus is the real reason of Christmas? Not to be mean, but he is. *Rosanne, 11*

—SUBMITTED BY ALAN KERR

How many elves does it take to change a lightbulb?

Ten. One to change the bulb, and nine to give him a boost.

At Purdue University, shortly before Christmas vacation, I saw a pair of pantyhose dangling from a window in one of the men's dorms. Then I realized that there were pantyhose hanging from almost every window. A sign on the building read: "Dear Santa, please fill these appropriately."

—LEZLIE DOUTHITT

On Christmas Eve my nine-year-old son, David, put out milk and cookies for Santa, plus an extra treat—a beer. The next morning, David came tearing into our room. "Santa came!" he shouted. Holding up the half-full bottle of beer, he said,

"See? There really is a Santa, because Dad would have drunk the whole thing!"

—KAREN BELLAMY

Because of my fluency in American Sign Language, I was hired to be a Santa Claus in a large suburban mall. My employer wanted to provide deaf children with a Santa who could communicate with them.

I sat for hours, performing for the children who came to visit. But none of them were deaf. Then two girls approached shyly. One explained that her sister was deaf and could not speak.

"What is your name?" I signed slowly.

"J-A-S-M-I-N-E," she replied with her fingers, grinning from ear to ear.

I was bubbling over with pride when I absentmindedly signed, "My name is H-E-N-R-Y. Nice to meet you."

The startled child pulled back and furiously began signing, "I thought your name was Santa Claus!"

—HENRY E. LOWE

Why does Santa Claus come down the chimney on Christmas Eve?

Because it soots him.

— CHRISTOPHER WALTER

My four-year-old was sitting on Santa Claus's knee at the shopping center and was asked, "And what's your name, little boy?"

Aghast, Adrian replied, "Don't you know?"

—ROSALIE NISSEN

"Santa, have you lost weight?" . . . "Mrs. Claus is looking exceptionally pretty." . . . "Your toys look wonderful this year."
—Rudolph's cousin, Larry the Brownnose Reindeer

—DAVE WEINBAUM

While doing some Christmas shopping, I overheard a clerk ask a young customer what he wanted Santa to bring him for Christmas. The little boy's face lighted up as he answered enthusiastically, "A baby brother." Upon hearing this request, his mother patted him on the head and replied sweetly, "I'm afraid there just aren't enough shopping days left, dear."

—DANNIE HAMMETT

When he returned home from his office, my husband, Peter-John, a small-town doctor, told me that one of his patients had handed him a letter and asked his advice on what she should do. The letter was from her small son, written to Santa Claus, and it read: "Dear Santa, please phone me. My number is . . ."

Later that night, I overheard Peter-John on the phone. In his deepest voice, he said: "Ho! Ho! Ho! Hello, Andrew! Do you know who this is?"

—JUDY PACE

I had wondered if my seven-year-old daughter was starting to doubt about whether there was a Santa—until Christmas Eve night. She woke up at 2:30 a.m. and again at 4:00 a.m. Each time she woke me up, I told her that if she didn't go back to sleep, Santa wouldn't come.

At 4:30 she could contain herself no longer. She woke me up and declared: "I can't take it! I've got to go see if I've been good!"

—COLLEEN V. GAZDEWICH

A coworker of mine, Cheryl, had done some last-minute shopping on Christmas Eve, leaving her two young sons with her husband. Over the course of the evening, the boys asked for some chocolate milk and Dad obliged, helping them mix the powder into their milk.

Later that night, Cheryl's unusually excited boys were in their parents' bedroom, almost hourly asking if Santa had arrived yet.

Cheryl learned why when a day or so later the boys asked her for some chocolate milk. She told them they had none. But they did, the boys insisted, and showed her what their Dad had made for them on Christmas Eve—Swiss Mocha coffee.

—BILL HARRISON

On a trip to see Santa, my friend's young son Danny climbed onto St. Nick's lap and shared his wish list. Later that day, in another store, there was Santa again.

"And what would you like for Christmas?" he asked Danny.

Shaking his head, Danny sighed, **"You really need to write these things down."**

—RUBY POPP

Oh, Christmas Tree!

Every December it was the same excruciating tradition. Our family would get up at the crack of dawn, go to a Christmas tree farm, and tromp across acres of snow in search of the perfect tree. Hours later our feet would be freezing, but Mom would press on, convinced the tree of her dreams was "just up ahead."

One year I snapped. "Mom, face it. The perfect tree doesn't exist. It's like looking for a man. Just be satisfied if you can find one that isn't dead, doesn't have too many bald spots, and is straight."

—CHRISTY MARTIN

Getting the lights on the Christmas tree can be a production that ranks right up there with hanging wallpaper. Throughout the process, I usually direct my husband as he secures the lights on each branch.

One Christmas, however, when we finally stood back and flicked on the light switch, I noticed that one branch obscured our prized angel ornament. I grabbed the pruning shears, mounted a stool, snipped once, and the lights went out. My ever patient husband, bless his heart, quietly said, "You don't have your glasses on, do you, dear?"

—LYNN KITCHEN

Knowing that my Jewish coworker, Morris, had married a Christian girl, I wondered how they would celebrate Christmas. As I approached their house, I could see reflections of a brightly lighted tree, and I knew that Morris's new wife had had her way. But Morris had the last word: The tree was topped by a brilliant Star of David.

—FRANCIS HANGARTER

"You gotta admit, it's straight now."

My brother Paulo decided to go camping with his family and asked his son and wife to get the box with the tent in the basement and put it in the car.

After a trip filled with great expectations, they arrived at the camping site and amidst great excitement they opened the tent box, from where a beautiful Christmas tree emerged.

—LUIZA AUGUSTA ROSSIGNOLLI SATO

At a Christmas tree lot in Toronto: **"Buy your wife a fir for Christmas."**

—MARY LE GROW

At first sight we knew it was the perfect Christmas tree. Tall, full and lush, and with no bare spots. Even our grown children were impressed.

"Wow," said my son, "if you didn't know it was real, it could easily pass as artificial."

—ROBERT PIEL

A customer walked into our store looking for Christmas lights. I showed her our top brand, but—wanting to make sure each bulb worked—she asked me to take them out of the box and plug them in. I did, and each one lit up.

"Great," she said.

I carefully placed the string of lights back in the box. But as I handed them to her, she looked alarmed.

"I don't want this box," she said abruptly. "It's been opened."

—GLENN PETTY

Just before Christmas, I was shopping at a local mall with my sister and her children. In the parking lot was a fellow selling Christmas trees from a camper trailer.

"Hey, look, Mom!" three-year-old Nick exclaimed. "That guy's camping. He even brought his own woods!"

—CHERYL GILLESPIE

Forget roses or ferns, Jay Leno tells guys on *The Tonight Show*. A Christmas tree is the perfect houseplant for them. "Because it's already dead," he explains, "you cannot screw it up more."

A Nashville grandfather took his four-year-old grandson out in the woods to select a Christmas tree. They tramped all over, but the boy couldn't find a tree that suited him. Finally, it began to get dark and cold, and the grandfather said they would have to quit looking.

"We'll have to take the next tree," he said flatly.

"Even if it doesn't have any lights either?" asked the boy.

—RED O'DONNELL, *NASHVILLE BANNER*

Some of my favorite childhood memories involve our family's annual trips to the local Christmas-tree farm. Although we have an artificial tree at our house, my children are still able to partake in the tradition by accompanying my parents when they cut down their tree.

When I announced we would be helping them pick a tree the following weekend, I expected Ethan, my six-year old, to be excited about the outing.

Instead, he furrowed his brow, puzzled, and asked, "What did they do with the one we got them last year?"

—SARA DAUB

One of my students told me she was happy because her family had got their Christmas tree the night before. "Is it real?" I asked.

"Yes," she replied, then paused for a second before continuing. **"Actually, I don't know. We haven't taken it out of the box yet."**

—TANIS MARSHALL

What Your Christmas Tree Says About You

- **White lights:** You ask houseguests to remove their shoes.
- **Multicolored lights:** You're an extrovert.
- **Blinking Lights:** You have attention deficit disorder.
- **Homemade ornaments:** You have lots of children.
- **Strung Popcorn:** You have too much time on your hands.
- **Red balls only:** You wish you lived in a department store.
- **Yellow star on top:** You're traditional.
- **Glowing Santa on top:** You shop at Kitsch 'R' Us.
- **Cutoff top:** You didn't measure the tree.
- **Vague evergreen smell:** You bought a healthy tree.
- **Strong evergreen smell:** You sprayed your tree with Pine-Sol.
- **Just plain smelly:** There's a dead bird in your tree.

—REBECCA MUNSTERER

You can tell a lot about a person by the way they handle these three things: rainy days, lost luggage, and tangled Christmas tree lights.

—EDWARD THOMPSON

I've always wanted a beautiful shawl to wear with my winter dresses. So when I opened the present from my sister Wanda and saw that it was a white-and-silver shawl, I squealed in delight.

"I love it!" I told Wanda that evening. "I wore it all morning."

"You wore it?" she asked, smiling. "It's a skirt for the Christmas tree."

—KAY PRZYBILLE

Sign on a Christmas-tree lot across the street from several posh shops in Troy, Michigan: **"Firs by Frederick."**

—DAVID W. CHUTE

An uncle of a friend of mine was reminiscing about Christmas during the Depression, when he was just a boy. "We couldn't afford fancy Christmas tree ornaments," he said wistfully, "so we had to settle for apples and oranges to decorate the tree."

Thinking nostalgically of the old days, my friend asked, "Would you like to do that this year?"

"Heck, no," came the answer. "Can't afford to."

—E. B. WINSTON

To decorate our Christmas tree, my eight-year-old daughter, Traci, wanted to string cranberries, so I sent my husband out to buy some for her.

I was putting up the tree when he returned with the cranberries. Not long after, I could hear Traci moaning and groaning that the cranberries wouldn't stay on the thread and her fingers were numb. After admonishing her a couple of times to stop complaining, that this was her idea, I finally turned around.

Cranberries were everywhere except on the thread, and juice was dripping off her hands. Her father had bought frozen cranberries.

—GRETA WOODCOCK

From the *Westfield* (Massachusetts) *Evening News* police log: "A caller reports that her neighbors are having another argument. The responding officer reports the resident was alone and not intoxicated but was having a disagreement with his Christmas tree, which was giving him trouble as he was taking it down."

—DOROTHY CUSSON

Deck the Halls with Office Follies

A waitress at our restaurant had a change of clothes stolen from the break room. Making matters worse, she'd planned on wearing them to the Christmas party.

As a brand-new employee, I didn't know any of this backstory, so I was a bit surprised to find this indignant note posted on the community board: "It has been two weeks since the Christmas party, and I still have not found my clothes."

—DAVID BUTTS

I share an office with three coworkers, one of whom loves to chat. She was scheduled to appear on a local TV show to promote our company's products as gift ideas for the Christmas holidays, and she was telling us about it.

"Eight minutes is a long time for an interview," she commented. "Imagine if I were to talk nonstop for the next eight minutes."

"I agree," one of my officemates replied. "It would feel like an eternity."

—ANITA HELMUS

As luck would have it, I drew the name of my principal at our school's Secret Santa Christmas party. A first-year teacher, I had no clue what to get her. I threw out a few ideas to some colleagues, but they always responded the same: "She already has one."

Desperate, I asked a doctor friend, "What do you give to a woman who has everything?"

He thought a moment before telling me what he gives in such situations: "Penicillin."

—DALE DAVIS

"I heard a rumor the boss may hand out holiday bonuses this year!"

Business merchant: **"Dashing through the dough."**

—RALPH M. WYSER

On the job as a legal secretary, I accompanied a lawyer to court just before Christmas. The attorney was representing a young defendant who was feeling very confident, almost cocky, obviously expecting leniency from the judge because of the season.

Suddenly the defendant started singing under his breath, "I'll Be Home for Christmas."

The judge, quick on his feet, sang back, "When You Wish Upon a Star." Our client waited for St. Nick behind bars.

—GEORGIA BENJAMIN

At our office Christmas party, a new female executive managed to break the ice and bridge the generation gap in one sentence. We had talked about how she would introduce her longtime live-in boyfriend to her boss, a conservative known to have strong opinions about the morality of the younger generation.

While she didn't intend to lie about her lifestyle, she also didn't want to jeopardize her position or embarrass anyone with views different from her own. When the time came for introductions, she led the young man to the boss and said, "I'd like you to meet Arthur Holt, my person to contact in case of emergency."

There was a slight pause. Then the boss laughed, shook the young man's hand, and invited the couple to join him in some holiday cheer.

—S.D.S.

Two executives, Gary and Bill, staggered out of their company's holiday party in New York City. Bill crossed the street, while Gary stumbled into a subway entrance. When Bill reached the other side, he noticed Gary emerging from the subway stairs. "Where've you been?" Bill slurred.

"I don't know," replied Gary, "but you should see the train set that guy has in his basement."

—WILLIAM ONORATO

The casino where I worked went through a round of layoffs just before the holidays. But it wasn't all bad news. In a memo, management stated, "During the Christmas season, laid-off casino employees will not have to wait the normal mandatory seven days before they are allowed to gamble."

—BOB TREBIL

In January my wife, a physician, met with an elderly patient. "So was Santa good to you?" she asked.

"Real good," he said. "I got an SUV."

"Nice."

"Yeah . . . socks, underwear, and Viagra."

—BRUCE NOBLE

The contest was simple: Which department in the hospital where I worked as a nurse could create the best Christmas decorations?

While they didn't win first prize, the members of the proctology department did receive high honors with their distinctive sign: **"Christmas is a good time to look up old friends."**

—PAT INGELS

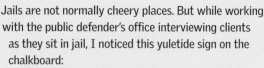

Jails are not normally cheery places. But while working with the public defender's office interviewing clients as they sit in jail, I noticed this yuletide sign on the chalkboard:

"Only 10 more shoplifting days till Christmas!"

—SUSAN CARMAN

Employer: "Here's the official letter on your raise, John. I hope you're satisfied with it."

John: "Thank you very much, Boss. And here's the tape recording of our last Christmas party."

—JOSEPH LOZANOFF

I know my company has made a big effort to be family friendly, but I was baffled when I read this holiday announcement posted on the bulletin board: "All employees are invited to the annual Christmas party. All children under the age of ten will receive a gift from Santa. Employees who have no children may bring grandchildren."

—KRISTIN BAYHAN

My mother writes a column for more than 200 newspapers, and Dad, now retired, helps her answer the mail. They follow a very businesslike procedure—I didn't realize how businesslike until last Christmas Eve. Mother was in her office, and Dad called her to the kitchen. When she came into the room, she saw an array of hors d'oeuvres and a bottle of champagne. "It's our office party," Dad explained, popping the cork.

—SUSAN M. STEIN

Announcement in our church bulletin: **"All singles are invited to join us Friday at 7 p.m. for the annual Christmas Sing-alone."**

—JENNIFER BURLEY

Our office Christmas party was a week away, and I had purchased a gorgeous off-the-shoulder floor-length gown for the occasion. But since the weather was so cold, I decided I would need something to cover my shoulders.

I was excited to discover several shawls at one store and went into the dressing room to try them on. One over-the-shoulder cape perfectly matched the material of my dress. However, there was something about it that seemed a bit odd, but I couldn't quite put my finger on it—until I looked at the tag. It read: "tree skirt."

—SHANNON FIDDLER

It was Christmastime, and I was having a difficult day running my home business. While I was downstairs working, our home phone rang. Since I had forgotten to bring the portable with me, I ran upstairs to answer it. The caller gave up while I was searching for the phone, so I called our home number from my business line to find the handset.

I finally located it when I heard one of my son's gifts ringing under the Christmas tree. I had wrapped the phone with it by mistake.

—DONNA RAUSCHENBERGER

Why is Christmas like a day in the office?
You do all the work and the fat guy in the suit gets all the credit.

The Art of Gifting

When I picked up my son at the airport a few days before Christmas, I was surprised to see him waiting with only his backpack—the airline had lost his luggage. After filling out some forms, we headed home, updating each other on what was new. Knowing he was the typical financially strapped student, I asked what he was giving his mother and brother for Christmas. "Well," he replied, "if they really have lost my bags, all my presents were in them. If they find them, then I have to go shopping tomorrow."

—GORD WADDINGTON

We spend most Christmases with my husband's family, so my mother celebrates Christmas with us two weeks earlier. Once, after a wonderful day opening presents, eating turkey, and seeing other family members, my mother handed me a present. "Please open this Christmas morning. I want you to have a gift to open from me," she said.

Even as a child, I'd never been able to wait to open a gift. With my mom's present, I really, really tried—but lasted two days. Finally, I unwrapped it, lifted the lid of the box, and read the note on top of the present: "What are you opening this for? It's not Christmas yet!"

—DONNA FORD

My 13-year-old grandson David was excited to learn his aunt had sent a check for his mother to buy Christmas presents for him and his brother. David craned his neck to see the check, which his mother hid, saying, "It's the thought that counts."

"I know," David replied. "I just want to see how big the thought was!"

—CAROL CHARTERS

My husband went to the mall with my "Dear Santa" list. One item was perfume. Not having a fragrance in mind, I'd written that I would like something subtle.

Hours later I got an exasperated call. "I'm having a very hard time finding Something Subtle," he told me. "The sales clerk wants to know who makes it."

—JEAN FITZGERALD

Our family drove to a nearby shopping center one morning to buy Christmas presents for one another. In order for the four of us to keep our purchases secret, we decided to split up and meet back at the car.

"Let's all synchronize our watches," Dad said, "so we'll be back here at the same time."

We adjusted our watches and were beginning to go our separate ways when Mom turned to Dad with her hand outstretched and said, "Now let's all synchronize our wallets!"

—BEVERLY BREWER

One week before Christmas, my wife, Theresa, and I discovered we'd each bought the same gift for each other—The Beatles' Number One CD. My wife suggested I return mine, but I suggested whoever paid the most for theirs should be the one to deal with the return.

After she told me how much she had paid—$18.99—I said, "Well, I paid only $16.99, so I guess you'll have to return yours."

"How could you get me such a cheap gift?" she asked indignantly.

—PAUL ROTH

"Don't make it look too nice, I want her to think I did it myself."

What I like about Christmas is that you can make people forget the past with the present.

—DON MARQUIS

My friend reviewed her young son's fill-in-the-blank homework.

One line: "At Christmas we exchange gifts with____."

His response: "Receipts."

—CAROL SCHNELL

Last autumn I found a bargain-priced pair of slippers, size 12, and gave them to my husband, David. But he said he didn't wear slippers, so I set them aside for our family's "White Elephant" gift exchange at Christmas.

The way it works at our get-togethers is you choose a gift marked "man" or "woman" from among the presents when your number is called. When the time came, I watched David choose the gift-wrapped box I had added to the pile. "Look at these nice slippers," he said to me after he opened it. "I can't believe they're the right size, too!"

—IRENE MYERS

My grandfather passed away not long before Christmas, and at almost the same time, my mother's friend lost a close relative.

When they exchanged presents a week later, Mom wrote a sensitive message on the gift tag: "May God give you peace at this difficult time."

Mom was expecting a note of condolence from her friend, but she had evidently chosen not to dwell on the bereavement: Mom's present—a hedgehog garden ornament—came with a tag bearing the words, "I hope you have room for him in your garden."

—MARK SHEARMAN

Last Christmas morning, after all the presents were opened, it was clear that my five-year-old son wasn't thrilled with the ratio of toys to clothes he'd received. As he trudged slowly up the stairs, I called out, "Hey, where are you going?"

"To my room," he said, **"to play with my new socks."**

—RICK BURNS

I spent days searching for the perfect Christmas gift for my husband. Finally, I decided on a hooded full-length purple terry robe and could see from his face on Christmas morning that I'd made the perfect choice. With great enthusiasm Ed put on his robe just as our youngest daughter walked into the room.

She stopped, stared, and said, "Why are you dressed like Barney?"

—LINDA ATMANIK

My four-year-old daughter Sarah received a Christmas gift from her pet goldfish. I could tell she was perplexed. At dinner she asked, "Dad, how did Happy get me a gift?"

Caught off guard, I improvised, "Well, Happy wanted to show you he loves you, so he got you a present."

Not satisfied, she pressed on, "Yeah, but how?"

I started conjuring up an elaborate tale about how Happy had done mail-order shopping, but changed tactics and put the ball back in her court. "Why do you find it strange that Happy would get you a gift?"

"Dad," she shot back, "everyone knows goldfish can't wrap."

—JOHN BARRY

For Christmas my niece and her husband bought a toy parrot that repeats everything you say. Trying it out, they accidentally knocked it off the table. It didn't look broken, but the wings would no longer flap. Hoping to return it to the store, my niece boxed it back up and advised her husband, "Don't tell the clerk it fell off the table; just tell him it was defective."

Immediately the bird inside the box began to chant, "Fell off the table! Fell off the table!"

—BECKY MCGLAUFLIN

One Christmas my husband put an assortment of beauty products in my stocking. I tried one of the facial masks and was about to wash it off when my eight-year-old son, Callum, walked in. I explained to him that it was a present from his Dad and it would make me beautiful.

He patiently waited by my side as I rinsed and patted my face dry. "Well, what do you think?" I asked.

"Oh, Mom, it didn't work!" Callum replied.

—LYNN THIBODEAU

Our daughters, Rebecca, 10, and Sabrina, 12, love to try to guess what their presents are by shaking them. On Christmas morning my wife secretly switched the tags on two gifts. The girls were thoroughly confused, until the truth was revealed and the presents they had predicted they would receive were in the right hands.

"What a relief," Rebecca said. "I thought that I was losing my powers!"

—BRIAN PRICE

Husband: **"On the twelfth day of Christmas, my true love gave to me—all the bills."**

At a variety store, I overheard this conversation between a husband and wife who were obviously rethinking their Christmas list.

"We've bought her a couple of gifts, but do you think she will have enough?"

"Well, I sure don't want her to feel left out."

"Maybe we should just forget it."

"No. I want to buy her just one more. Which do you think she'd rather have, a new collar or one of these chewy bones?"

—ROBERT F. DANNER

I received a box of chocolates for Christmas, and as sweets were abundant in the house, I placed it in the freezer to be enjoyed later.

Recently, longing for some chocolate, I rooted around in the freezer and finally spied the holiday box. I lifted it out, opened it, and found that I'd preserved a plaid scarf and gloves.

—HELEN FLAIG

A friend and his wife decided that letting their young son open all his gifts at once on Christmas morning always turned into present overload. So last December they decided to hold back the big gift—a bike—until after lunch. Unable to figure out how to wrap it, they tied a balloon to the handlebars.

Christmas Day arrived, lunch was eaten, and then the boy's mother announced, "Look what else Santa brought you." And with that, my friend wheeled in the bike.

"Yippee," the boy shouted. "A balloon!"

—JIM WATT

"There's nothing in any of them.
Like he's going to know the difference."

I was going shopping to buy a gift for my wife and asked for her sizes. "If it's clothes, I wear small," she said. "If it's diamonds, I wear large."

—WENDELL W. FENN

Pre-Christmas payments of application fees to several graduate schools had left my son Brian's bank balance low. On Christmas morning each member of the family received a token gift from him, along with a card carrying the following announcement: "Congratulations! In lieu of a gift, a graduate school has been applied to in your honor." The name of a different school was written on each card.

—DOROTHY G. JONES

I thought it would be nice to send a Christmas package to my in-laws in Florida. I went shopping at a local department store and found the perfect gift to send: gourmet coffee, shortbread, and a selection of jams in a festive candy-cane basket.

I called my in-laws on Christmas Day to wish them a merry Christmas. They told me that instead of festive jams, I had sent body frosting complete with a set of instructions.

—BLAIR MCLAUGHLIN

In our home we celebrate Hanukkah, but in keeping with the holiday spirit, my husband and I delivered a box of cookies to a neighbor, saying, "Ho! Ho! Ho! And a very merry Christmas!"

Two days later the neighbor's two children stopped by to reciprocate. The mother had coached her children with the proper greeting, so when I opened the door, the four-year-old handed me a gaily wrapped package and proudly exclaimed, "Merry Christmas and a happy harmonica!"

—ROBERTA COLETON

At day care my grandson and the other children drew names for a gift exchange. When he got home, Mitchell asked his mother to read him the piece of paper.

"It says that you got Christopher's name for Christmas," she said.

Mitchell looked uneasy. "Will everyone call me Christopher from now on?"

—HAZEL HUSZAR

Doing my Christmas shopping, when I was stationed at one of our continental Marine Corps air stations, I ran across a toy bagpipe. It seemed an ideal present for the young son of one of my brother officers on the base, so I sent it to him with a card: "Love to Peter from Uncle Jock."

About 10:00 on Christmas morning, I was awakened by a knock on my door at bachelor officers quarters. There stood my young friend, dressed in his Sunday best, with suitcase and bagpipe. From his neck hung a card: "To Uncle Jock, with love from Peter's parents."

—JOHN T. L. D. GABBERT

Our oldest son had his heart set on a new two-wheeler for Christmas, and our youngest wanted a tricycle. Money was tight, so we decided to buy a bicycle and fix up the old red tricycle as a gift for son number two.

One night I brought the trike in from our driveway and set to work. Four hours later a gleaming blue wonder stood there, complete with new pedals, handle grips, seat, and tires. Just then my wife came into the garage with a funny expression on her face. She was pushing another old red three-wheeler. I had worked my Christmas "miracle" on a tricycle belonging to the child next door.

—WILLIAM R DRUMMOND

" . . . And our 'Holiday Scented' candle smells just like credit cards. "

Sign in department store: **"Make this a Christmas he won't forget—charge everything."**

—WINTON BURRHUS

My six-year-old daughter had chosen the perfect Christmas present for me at a craft sale early in November. When it was time to put our presents under the tree, she found everything she had hidden, except the gift for me. "I don't know what could have happened to it, Mommy," she said. "I put it where I thought you'd never look."

"Where did you put it?" I asked.

"In the garbage can," she replied.

—JANET ROBINSON

We bought my mother a shelf for Christmas, and I asked my husband if he'd hang it as part of her gift.

"Sure," he agreed. "Just remind me to take my tools."

I scribbled a note and stuck it on the gift.

"Holidays getting you down, Mom?" my daughter said.

She pointed to my Post-it: "Take items to hang self."

—BEVERLY WOLF

All the family gathered around the Christmas tree, and as the magic moment for present distribution arrived, wrapping paper was torn asunder and oohs and aahs greeted each gift.

Mom had chosen a box containing two exquisite silk ties for Dad, and rather than saying a simple "Thank you, dear," he quietly slipped away to their bedroom. There he changed from his casual attire into a crisp white shirt and his best suit before parading in front of Mom wearing one of the ties.

She looked at the tie, then asked, "Don't you like the other one?"

—WINSTON WADE

When I found out the price of the lovely powder-blue dressing gown my husband gave me for Christmas, I took it back to the store to exchange it for two less expensive ones. The clerk to whom I explained what I had in mind stared at me wide-eyed.

"Was that man really your husband?"

"Yes, of course," I replied. "Why?"

She called to another girl, "Remember the man who had you model all those robes? Well, he really was buying it for his wife! Imagine!" Turning to me, she asked, "How long have you been married?"

"Twenty-seven years."

The girl shook her head. "Lady, if I were you I wouldn't exchange that robe for anything. I've been selling a long time, and I never saw a man who chose a gift for his wife with such care. You sure are lucky."

I really enjoy wearing that robe.

—RUTH JOHNSON

My husband doesn't buy me intimate apparel, so I was delighted when his grandmother sent me a semi-slinky nightie for Christmas. Meanwhile, he received a much-needed set of plastic storage drawers, which he put to use right away.

He expressed his appreciation to his grandmother in these words: **"I have filled the drawers and emptied the nightie. Thank you for both!"**

—TANIA LEIGH

Rummaging through eBay, I came across these items for sale, along with their descriptions:

- Gilded plate: "Plate has small chip and lots of guilt."

- Ceramic lion: "One of the prettiest loins you'll ever see."

- Fake Christmas tree: "X-mas tree will tinkle with the push of a button."

—SANDRA HUFF

Just before their second Christmas as a couple, my sister and her husband were discussing their wish lists. "Do you remember the lovely drill bits you gave me last year?" he asked

"Do you think that this year I could get the drill?"

—JACQUELINE MCGANN

The quilt store where my wife, Donna, shops has a men's shopping night before Christmas, where husbands can fill their wives' wish lists. Last year I attended, and this year, to keep Donna's gift a surprise, I pretended I had a prior engagement the night of the sale.

That night, I stopped at the quilt store, bought Donna a Christmas present, and entered a door-prize draw.

The next day, when I got home from work, Donna said I had a phone message. We listened to the message together: I won a prize at the quilt store the night before.

—HUGH WOLLIS

Did you hear about the dyslexic devil worshipper?

He sold his soul to Santa.

Shortly before Christmas, I almost stumbled over a little boy in the middle of the sidewalk who was so busy playing with a toy merry-go-round, a waddling duck, and a walking man that he was oblivious to the crowd milling around him. His obvious pleasure made me think the same toys would delight my own youngster. I asked the little boy where he got them.

"In there," he said, pointing to a shop behind him.

I went in and asked for the toys the small boy was playing with. "Who is he?" I asked as the proprietor wrapped my purchases.

She smiled. "You might say he's my Christmas present. A few days ago he came in and stood staring longingly at the merry-go-round. 'Would you like it for Christmas?' I asked. 'Mother says there isn't any money for Christmas this year. We lost Dad last spring,' he explained, and turned to go.

"It had been a lean season for me—but it was the week before Christmas. I gave him the merry-go-round, and he was so delighted that he got no farther than the sidewalk before he sat down and wound it up. Then the most amazing thing happened. People stopped to talk to him—and I've never had so many customers. I kept count of the merry-go-rounds I sold, and when he got up to go, I called him in and gave him a twenty-five percent commission. I asked him to come back the next day and added the duck and the man to his playthings. Yesterday his commission amounted to eleven dollars!"

—G. C. HENLEY

QUOTABLE QUOTES

"There is a remarkable breakdown of taste and intelligence at Christmastime. Mature, responsible grown men wear neckties made of holly leaves and drink alcoholic beverages with raw egg yolks and cottage cheese in them."

—P.J. O'ROURKE

"Guilt: the gift that keeps on giving."

—ERMA BOMBECK

"Oh, volunteer work! That's what I like about the holiday season. That's the true spirit of Christmas. People being helped by people other than me."

—JERRY SEINFELD

"Oh, joy, Christmas Eve. By this time tomorrow, millions of Americans, knee-deep in tinsel and wrapping paper, will utter those heartfelt words: 'Is this all I got?'"

—KELSEY GRAMMER ON *FRASIER*

"The main reason Santa is so jolly is because he knows where all the bad girls live."

—GEORGE CARLIN

"No matter how carefully you stored the lights last year, they will be snarled again this Christmas."

—ROBERT KIRBY
IN THE *SALT LAKE TRIBUNE*

"Christmas: It's the only religious holiday that's also a federal holiday. That way, Christians can go to their services, and everyone else can sit at home and reflect on the true meaning of the separation of church and state."

—SAMANTHA BEE

"What I don't like about office Christmas parties is looking for a job the next day."

—PHYLLIS DILLER

"Where's your little brother?"

The Very Merry Things Kids Say

Just before Christmas, my five-year-old grandson, Jacob, said, "Could you put away all the decorations, Dad? I want Christmas to be over with."

"But why?" asked his father.

"I'm just so tired of being good!"

—DAVID GRIFFITHS

"You know, I'm not sure I believe in Santa Claus anymore," said my five-year-old nephew a few days before Christmas.

"Oh!" I said laconically, unsure how to respond to this revelation that surely marked a turning point in Louis's existence.

Without reacting to my slight uncertainty, my nephew continued his line of thought: "Almost every time I ask him for something, he sends it to me. So I think I'll go on believing in him for one more year."

—JEAN LAMBERT

Early in December I was racing madly around the house to get my three boys dressed for a children's Christmas party. I wanted them to look just so for their picture with Santa. I was proud of the results when I inspected them before leaving.

Then my middle son piped up, "Aren't we supposed to wear underpants to parties?"

—DENISE SEMOS

A little girl was saying her prayers in a very loud voice and adding what she'd like from Father Christmas. "You needn't shout," her mother admonished her. "God isn't deaf."

"I know," her daughter replied, "but Grandma is."

—PAT ELPHINSTONE

Four-year-old to her two-year-old sister: **"Let's play Christmas. I'll be Santa Claus, and you be a present and I'll give you away."**

—MRS. KENNETH LABAUGH

One Christmas I was teaching a class of ten-year-olds. We talked about how important it was to send cards to people who might be lonely.

The pupils were absorbed in silent contemplation, so I pressed on and asked, "What about giving a card to someone you don't even like very much?"

The children pondered this for a minute or so before one girl walked up to my desk, handed me an envelope, and said, "Merry Christmas, sir."

—UNKNOWN

My five-year-old son, Jordan, had been asking for an Easy-Bake oven for months, so when he received money for Christmas from his grandparents, I told him he could use the money to buy it.

The following week, we purchased the oven, and then we stopped by the grocery store to pick up the turkey.

"Don't worry about Christmas dinner, Mom," Jordan said excitedly. "I'll do the turkey!"

—KAREN LUCIAK

For 98 percent of the students at the school where my wife teaches, English is a second language. But that didn't stop them from giving her Christmas cards. Still, their enthusiasm for the occasion sometimes exceeded their grasp of English. Among the many cards that flooded her desk were: "Happy Birthday, Grandma," "Get Well Soon," and "Congratulations on Passing Your Driving Test!"

—JOHN HYDE

On the afternoon of Christmas Eve, one of my four daughters, Lizann, wanted to show me what she had bought for Holly, her youngest sister. We went to her room while the other girls got ready for the evening church service.

While we were sitting on the bed, door closed, looking at the gifts, Holly came to the door, wanting to come in. We told her she couldn't.

"But I have to ask you something," she said.

"Ask me through the door!" Lizann yelled.

After a moment, Holly called out, "How do I look?"

—SANDY GAGNON

One evening I arrived home from work to find the lights out. My wife had prepared a lovely candlelit dinner, and our two young sons, Garett and Seldon, were dressed in their suits.

"Hey," I joked, "didn't we pay our hydro bill?"

A few months later, during the Christmas Eve candlelit procession, the church was packed and silent when Garett asked, "Hey, Dad, did they not pay their hydro bill, too?"

—SYLVIO GRAVEL

On the last day of school before Christmas vacation, I sent my son to the bus stop with a box of chocolates for the driver. Three weeks later I was getting his school bag ready to return to classes when I unearthed the box. "Why didn't you give the driver her chocolates?" I quizzed.

"I did, Mom," he protested. **"I gave her one!"**

—LYNN AUBIN

When my niece was a student, her class of six-year-olds sang, "Hark, the Herald Angels Sing" at a Christmas concert. The line "God and sinners reconciled" was a tricky one for this age group.

One little boy, with a voice that completely drowned out the rest of the choir, happily belted out, "God and sinners dressed in style!"

—JESSIE ROBERTSON

A few days before Christmas, just as we were about to leave for the visitation at the funeral home, we tried to explain to our children what had happened to Nana.

"Wow!" exclaimed four-year-old Alex. "Nana picked a good time to die." When he saw our confused faces, he explained, "She's going to heaven just in time for Jesus's birthday party."

We were humbled by his sweet response. "You know," he continued, "there are only four very, very lucky people invited to Jesus's birthday party."

"Who are the four?" we asked.

"You know, Nana and the Three Wise Men."

—ANGELICA HILDEBRAND

Our four-year-old son, Gerald, was thrilled with the electric train set he got for Christmas. As I was in the kitchen preparing dinner, I heard him say, "Dad, isn't it neat that I got an electric train from Santa?"

My husband, busily getting the train set up, did not respond. Then I heard Gerald say, "Dad, isn't it neat that we got an electric train from Santa?"

My husband still did not respond. Then Gerald said, "Dad, isn't it neat that you got an electric train from Santa?" I laughed so loudly, my husband finally looked up.

—WILMA VAN DUNGEN

"Come on, Rusty . . . you know they mixed up our presents."

"What is Christmas a time for?" I asked my Sunday school class. Came the usual answers: Jesus's birthday, a time of joy, a time for presents, etc.

But one 11-year-old's answer was unique: "Christmas is a time for sportsmanship, because you don't always get everything you want."

—DONALD POSTEN

My mother cast one of her students as the innkeeper for the Christmas pageant. All the third-grader had to do was tell Joseph, "There is no room at the inn."

But during the performance—after Joseph begged for a room for his pregnant wife—the boy didn't have the heart to turn him down.

"Well," he said, **"if it's so urgent, come on in."**

—ALEX DOMOKOS

When my son, Terrence, was four years old, he piqued everyone's interest when he placed a childishly wrapped package under the tree for each family member.

On Christmas morning, Terrence looked on with joy and expectation as we opened his gifts. There were exclamations of "I thought I'd lost that!" and "So that's where that went!"

When we asked Terrence why he had wrapped our favorite items, he replied, "Because I knew it was something you would really want!"

—SANDI REIMER

I was watching television, and my seven-year-old brother was reading aloud the Christmas list he was sending to Santa Claus. "I would like a Pokémon video game and some Pokémon cards . . ." His voice became louder and louder, until he was almost screaming.

"Jack," I said, "you don't have to scream. Santa can hear you anyway."

"I know," he replied, "but it's better if Dad hears me, too."

—MICHAEL VEZINA

About a week before Christmas, I found signs that mice had got into the house. Each night before bed, I put down traps to try to catch the intruders. On Christmas Eve, as I went to get the traps, my daughter Josephine said, "You don't need to do that tonight, Dad."

"Why not?" I asked.

"Well, after all," she replied, "it's the night before Christmas."

—PETER J. PERRIN

For Christmas I gave my six-year-old nephew, Josh, a pair of *Iron Man* pajamas. Later in the evening, while helping him put them on, I asked if he liked them.

"I would wear anything you gave me, Auntie!" Josh exclaimed. "Except a bra!"

—JANICE HICKEY

During Christmas shopping, my son, Daniel, lost his wallet. I learned how different his reaction was to losing a wallet, compared with me.

"Oh, no!" he said. "Someone might use my library card, return the books late, and not pay the late fee."

—GARY O'LEARY

It was Judy's first Christmas pageant, and like all five-year-olds, she was thrilled to be in the manger scene. She came onstage clutching her gift and gazed in awe at the scene before her: Mary, Joseph, the resplendent wise men, shepherds, animals, all grouped around the simple cradle. Her face shone with eagerness as she approached the crib, and her eyes grew wide in wonder. With uncontainable joy she turned toward the congregation and called out: "Mommy, Daddy—Mary's had her baby. It's a boy!"

—ROBERT A. DOUGLAS

Every Christmas, my father makes a large and complex nativity scene with moss, branches, and many clay figures. He is as meticulous about it as he is with the garden. In fact, when my younger cousins came over, he would spend the whole afternoon outside making sure nobody stepped on the grass or flowerbeds.

One Christmas he caught my younger cousin leaning over the nativity scene removing figures from the moss and placing them in the sand path leading to the stable where baby Jesus was born.

"What's going on here?" he asked.

To which my cousin replied serenely: "You said you didn't want anybody stepping on the grass!"

—GONÇALO PIMENTEL SERRA

Even after they moved to their own homes, both our daughters and their families would either stay at our place Christmas Eve or arrive early Christmas morning to open Santa's gifts.

Last Christmas, during the opening of gifts, our telephone rang. We asked our oldest daughter, Jennifer, to grab it, as she was closest to the phone. She picked it up and walked into the hallway, where it was a bit quieter. Suddenly we heard a crash as the phone fell off the end table.

"Good grief!" Jennifer exclaimed. "It has a cord!"

—JIM MCLEAN

I phoned my four-year-old grandson Tyler shortly after Christmas and asked him what his favorite gift was.

"A drum set, Nan. Want to hear me play?"

He dropped the phone and started banging. After a few long minutes he returned. "Did you hear me play, Nan?"

"Yes, Tyler," I said. "But Nan is phoning long distance."

"It's okay," he reassured me. "I can come closer to the phone."

—MAUREEN PERRY

When school resumed after the Christmas break, my aunt asked my eight-year-old cousin: "Who is mom's dearest son that's going to do very well in school next term?"

To which my cousin immediately answered: "I'm the dearest son, but I don't know who is going to do very well at school."

—CATARINA FERNANDES

Just before Christmas, my son asked,
"Is there really a Santa Claus?" As he was in sixth grade,
I felt he was ready for the truth, so I told him.
Later, at bedtime, I asked how he was feeling.

"I'm sad," he said, tears welling up, "but I'm glad I know the truth. If I didn't and had kids someday, they wouldn't get anything."

—LYNN WINTER

In our house, Advent begins with the family assembling a Nativity scene on our mantel. We unwrap figurines one by one from their storage box and set them in place while retelling the story of the first Christmas, and we conclude by singing, "Away in a Manger."

The year our son, Douglas, was four, we finished and stood back to admire the angels, shepherds, Wise Men, animals, and Holy Family.

"But Mommy," Douglas complained, "you forgot the fish."

"The fish?" I responded. "What fish?"

"You know, Mommy," he said. "A whale in a manger."

—MARGARET HAMMOND

"That's my list so far. But be sure to check my Twitter updates for any changes."

While my five-year-old son Caleb played in his nightly bath, I quizzed him on a new book for "young and inquiring minds" that he had received for Christmas.

"What's the difference between a caribou and a reindeer?" I asked.

"That's easy, Mom," he replied. "Reindeer fly."

—DIANE WHITE

Close to Christmas, I arrived at the babysitter's one day to pick up my five-year-old daughter, Kelly, only to learn that she had been bouncing around on the furniture and had broken the coffee table. She seemed remorseful on the way home and asked me, "Will Santa Claus know?" I said I didn't think so.

"Will God know?" she then asked.

"God knows everything," I replied.

She thought for a moment, then asked, "Does God know Santa Claus?"

—PAT CONNOLLY

On the way to our children's school Christmas performance, our six-year-old daughter was uncharacteristically quiet. As we approached the school, she announced: "I don't really know my lines, so you might want to watch another kid."

—IAN TISDALE

Before the Christmas gathering of our French class, each student had written what he or she wanted most in the world on a slip of paper for the grab bag. When gifts were exchanged, many got cardboard models of sports cars or fake airline tickets. But a student who had requested an A in French unwrapped his gift to find this sign: "Freanch."

—PHILLIP F. KING

Corey, my seven-year-old son, asked me why people celebrate Christmas. Wanting him to know there are many religions, I began to explain that some people do not have Christmas.

"I know," he interrupted me, and in a world-weary tone stated, "I know. Some people celebrate Harmonica."

—JERRY WAUGHTAL

Our daughter was chosen to play the role of Mary in a Christmas pageant. The morning of the first rehearsal, we overslept and got her there late.

The director wearily dismissed our apologies. "It doesn't matter," he said. "The shepherds have hockey practice, and Joseph went ice fishing."

—T. BRADLEY HAYS

I was packing away Christmas ornaments in their boxes when my three-year-old son, Dylan, sat down beside me. Out of the blue, he asked me if we had bought our house. I thought it an odd question, but I said yes, we had bought it.

"Was it new when we bought it?" he wanted to know.

"Brand new," I answered.

Eyes huge, Dylan asked, "Where's the box?"

—MARY LEWIS

Helping me sort clothes into "save" and "give away" piles, my six-year-old daughter came across a garter belt. "What's this?" she asked.

"It's a garter belt," I said. Seeing that meant nothing to her, I added, "It's for holding up stockings."

"Ah," she said, carefully placing it in the "save" pile. "We'll use it Christmas Eve."

—NANCY HALL

It was December 21, and I was frantically preparing for Christmas. All day I complained that I didn't have time to do everything I had planned.

My four-year-old son watched me come and go as he played in front of the TV. Suddenly a TV announcer commented that this was the shortest day of the year.

Sébastien stopped playing and said to me with great compassion: "Oh, Mom, you're really not lucky!"

—FRANCE RODRIGUE-TESSIER

The hymnbooks in our church are designated G or R, depending on the color of their covers (green or red). As we were waiting for the service to begin on Christmas Eve, our nine-year-old son was reading the bulletin. He turned to his uncle and said, "We can't sing the hymns today; they're rated R."

—PATRICIA KIM

Last Christmas one father gave his boy a battery-operated tank, a battery-operated gun, and a battery-operated train. The child loved them. All day he sat around trying to make towers out of the batteries.

—ROBERT ORBEN

In fourth grade my daughter had to write a 200-word essay. She chose the subject "My Grandma, My Heroine." I suggested she e-mail a copy to her grandma, which she did immediately, adding this postscript:

"Did you get my Christmas wish list last week?"

—YOKE KENNEDY

What do you call a reindeer wearing earmuffs?

Anything you want—he can't hear you.

Visiting Montreal with my daughter Morgane, age 5, we silently entered Notre-Dame church and stopped in front of a statue of Christ.

"Who is that man?" she asked.

"Jesus," I replied.

"That's impossible!" she exclaimed. "At Christmas he was only a baby."

—VALÉRIE ANZALONE

At Christmas I took my son and my four-year old niece to the church to see the manger. There were the three Wise Men, numerous shepherds with their sheep, and a lot of ordinary people. Baby Jesus, Saint Joseph, and the Virgin Mary had an arch over their heads to symbolize halos. I heard my son say to his cousin: "Have you noticed that not all of them have a satellite dish?"

—MARIA EMÍLIA NOGUEIRA MARTINS

All my relatives know that I refold the wrapping paper from my Christmas presents for reuse later.

"Auntie," asked one of my young nieces, "why do you save all that paper?"

"I'm doing what's best for the environment," I replied, "so I'm recycling."

"Good thing you didn't ask that question five years ago," my daughter interrupted. "Then she was just plain cheap."

—OKSANNA GUDZ

On a drive home from visiting family over the holidays, my children and I stopped off at a corner store. The cashier turned to my four-year-old daughter and asked, "Was Santa good t' ya?"

My five-year-old son, not used to the Ottawa Valley accent, piped up, "Her name's not Tia."

—TRISTA FENNELL

I live next door to a four-year-old girl named Jayla. After Christmas she was showing her grandmother the new nativity scene they had gotten.

"These are the kings, Grandma," she said. "They brought Jesus gifts."

"Oh, how nice of them," said her grandma. "What did they bring?"

"Banana bread," Jayla replied.

—ESTHER PALFY

While Christmas shopping with my two young kids, I found myself listening to an enthusiastic preschooler singing Christmas carols in front of us in the checkout line.

"On the first day of Christmas, my true love gave to meeeee," he sang, "a bar fridge in a bare treeeee!"

—KATRINA BATEY

Our discussions at home about politics and world affairs had more impact on our children than we realized. At the end of our church's Christmas Eve service, the minister leaned across the pulpit to address the restless youngsters in the congregation: "Who is the good-natured, plump man who goes all over the world on Christmas Eve working miracles?"

Our ten-year-old son answered, "Henry Kissinger!"

—JUDITH B. AYERS

During the holidays, one fourth-grade class wrote, directed, and acted in a Christmas pageant at the second Presbyterian Church in Charleston, South Carolina. It opened with the scene at the inn. Joseph and Mary ask for a room overlooking Bethlehem.

Innkeeper: "Can't you see the 'No Vacancy' sign?"

Joseph: "Yes, but can't you see that my wife is expecting a baby any minute?"

Innkeeper: "Well, that's not my fault."

Joseph: "Well, it's not mine, either!"

—ASHLEY COOPER

I was surprised when my teenage son handed me a Christmas gift, because I knew he had little money to spend. Opening the wrapped box, I found two AA batteries with a note: "gift not included."

—CHET ROGOWSKI

Our daughter chose to go to college 1,400 miles away from home. As Christmas approached, we decided to dispense with gifts for one another so we could send her the airfare to spend the holidays with us. At the close of the joyous visit, we asked our daughter to phone us when she got back to college.

Our teenage son answered the phone that evening. I asked, "Who is it?"

He replied, "The Grinch who stole Christmas."

—MRS. W. B. LOWE

When my former landlady stopped by to visit one day, she told me about a group of Boy Scouts who had come to see her at the masonic home during the holidays. One boy said, "Mrs. B, you are my troop's problem for this Christmas."

—MRS. W. O. CAMPBELL

"Be careful opening it. He doesn't like being cooped up so long."

We had moved to Seattle from Texas, and each of us missed our old home. That December, when I went to pick up our first-grade son, Madison, from school, his teacher told me about a conversation she overheard.

One boy said, "We're Catholic, and we are going to Christmas Mass."

"We're Jewish," said another child. "And we're going to have a Hanukkah celebration."

Madison chimed in, "We're Texans, and we're going to have a barbecue."

—STEVE MOORE

When my four-year-old son got home from school, I asked him what he'd done that day. He told me that he'd learned a new Christmas song called "Dick the Horse."

"I've never heard of that one," I said, and asked him to sing it for me.

Taking a deep breath, he began to sing, *"Dick the horse with boughs of holly, fa la la la la la la . . ."*

—P. SECCOMBE

When my daughter, Laura, was three, she wanted a violin for Christmas more than anything in the world, and we were successful in finding one for her.

She unwrapped the instrument with great pleasure, then tucked it under her tiny chin, serious and solemn. She slowly ran the bow across the strings, and there was a squeal of discord. She looked up at us in surprise: **"Where's the music?"**

—KERRIN MONIZ

Elementary teachers in Nome, Alaska, subscribe to the same professional publications as their colleagues in other states, but their problems are sometimes different. The third-grade teacher, a newcomer to Alaska, had just received her latest project magazine and was discussing with the class the suggestions for a Christmas pageant. For the children playing Santa's reindeer, there should be brown cambric outfits, and passable reindeer horns could be made of bare branches, trimmed to the proper shapes and painted. She looked out at the barren, treeless landscape.

"Well, children," she sighed regretfully, "I guess we'll have to do something else. We can't make horns of branches, because there isn't a tree for miles."

The children looked disappointed. Then one little boy spoke up. "We haven't any trees, teacher," he said, "but we do have lots of reindeer horns."

—EDITH M. JARRETT

On Christmas morning I was telling the story of the Nativity to a group of youngsters in an armed forces Sunday school. To test their attentiveness, I began to ask questions. Expecting a reply of either "the shepherds" or "the wise men," I asked, "Who was the first to know of Jesus's birth?"

Immediately a five-year-old waved her hand and shouted, "Mary!"

—JAMES L. JENSEN

My small daughter was addressing Christmas cards to a few carefully selected girls in her class at school. Casually I suggested, "Why don't you send a card to everyone in your class? That's the democratic thing to do."

"Why?" she exclaimed, looking up from her writing in surprise. "I thought being nice like that was republican."

—MARTHA WOLFE

Our seven-year-old son received a set of two-way radios for his birthday. On several occasions he has breathlessly reported picking up the conversations of helicopter pilots, truck drivers, etc., with the set. A few evenings before Christmas, on his way home from the office, my husband had one of the units in the car with him, and I had the other one turned on at home, with our son nearby.

As my husband neared home, he began saying, "Ho, ho, ho, Richard, this is Santa Claus."

After several "Ho, ho, hos" with no results, there was heard a very distinct reply: "Ho, ho, ho, license tag 18w 1678, this is not Richard. This is police car 67 behind you, and you are doing a pretty fair job of driving with one hand. Merry Christmas."

—CAROL T. DEBOEST

After listening to Christmas carols interspersed with news broadcasts on the radio, my three-year-old recited this version of 'Twas The Night Before Christmas: "Now Dasher, now Dancer, Prancer and Vixen! On Comet, on Cupid and President Nixon!"

—MARCELLA LECKY

While lounging in the battalion aid station one evening, I suddenly realized that Christmas in the jungles of South Vietnam was going to be a meaningless and depressing event. My melancholy was interrupted when the company clerk walked in dragging a mail sack bulging with Christmas cards.

"Grab one, sir," he said. "They're all addressed to the unit from people back in the states."

I picked up an envelope that had fallen to the floor and casually opened it. As I read the labored penmanship, I felt my spirits brighten and Christmas became merry indeed, for the moment. The card said: "Dear soldier, if you think things are bad there, I just got my report card. Good luck, Terry. Fourth grade."

—JOHN C. ANDREONI

Sitting at the kitchen table one evening in December, I told my husband, "I can't seem to get into the holiday spirit. I feel there is something I have to do, but I don't know what it is."

My seven-year-old son piped up, **"Maybe you should vacuum."**

—JACKIE WHITE

One day after church I asked our three-year-old daughter about the lessons and music she had learned that day. She told me they were singing Christmas songs. I was puzzled, because this was Easter, so I asked her to sing one.

In her clear voice she sang: "Ho-Santa, Ho-Santa!"

—PATTI HINZ

During the Christmas holidays, my niece, Justine, who had been staying with us, asked me, "Who is older, Grandpa or Grandma?"

I replied, "Grandpa is older. Why do you ask?"

"Well, if Grandpa is older," said Justine with a confused look on her face, "how come he always follows what Grandma says?"

—REYNANTA FERNANDEZ

My 11-year-old son had the role of Joseph in the Sunday-school Christmas program. We were discussing what he should wear on his feet. I suggested sandals, but he wanted to wear his cowboy boots. When I said it was unlikely that Joseph wore western boots, my son replied, "Yes, but then he didn't have braces on his teeth, either." He wore the boots.

—MRS. ROBERT D. OLSON

Ringing in the New Year

"An optimist stays up until midnight to see the New Year in. A pessimist stays up to make sure the old year leaves."

—BILL VAUGHAN

"This year just flew by."

✳ ✳ ✳ ✳ ✳ ✳ ✳ ✳ ✳ ✳ ✳ ✳

The Big Night

My mother-in-law was going to spend the holidays with us. Before her arrival, my husband, Barrie, and I debated whether or not she should accompany us to a party on New Year's Eve. Barrie wanted her to attend, but I worried she might feel out of place.

I turned to my 21-year-old son, who had been listening. "I agree with you, Mom," he said. "You shouldn't take her."

Surprised, as he always agrees with his dad, I was basking in his approval, when he added, "That would be like me taking you to a party with me."

—BEV FERGUSON

At a New Year's Eve celebration, tycoon to waiter about to fill his glass: "No, thank you. I do all my celebrating at the end of the fiscal year."

—UNKNOWN

On New Year's Eve at the turn of the millennium, our four-and-a-half-year-old little girl got very sleepy. So I said to her, "Don't go to sleep, Sandy. We'd so like to enter the new millennium with you!"

Half asleep, Sandy replied, "You go on ahead. I'll come after you on my bike!"

—MRS. GÁBOR TÓTH

On New Year's Eve we raised our champagne glass to the new year. A few weeks later my partner's daughter asked him for juice in one of the glasses we had used that night. Luc didn't understand what she meant, so she explained: "You know, Daddy. The pretty glasses with the high heels."

—SOPHIE GUÉNETTE

＊ ＊ ＊ ＊ ＊ ＊ ＊ ＊ ＊ ＊ ＊ ＊ ＊

Anything goes on New Year's Eve. It's when old acquaintances are forgot—along with hats, coats, and wives.

—ROBERT ORBEN

The hostess at a New Year's Eve party was blond, beautiful, buxom—and in a low-cut gown. My husband and another man sat on a sofa watching as she passed the fortune cookies. Bending low, she treated them to quite a spectacular view.

When my husband broke open his cookie, he convulsed with laughter. Wiping his eyes, he passed his fortune to me. It read: "One good look is worth 10,000 words."

—MRS. PAUL O. SNYDER

On New Year's Eve my neighbor telephoned her newlywed daughter—and was surprised to find her at home. "I thought you and Doug would be out celebrating," she said.

"No, Mom," her daughter replied. "We spent the day painting our bedroom. Then I put on the hostess gown you gave me for Christmas, Doug put on his tux, I set the table with our good china and silver, and we dined by candlelight. After dinner we changed our clothes and started painting again. It's been a wonderful evening!"

—JACK JOYCE

My husband and I hardly ever had an opportunity to stay out late. Having outgrown parents' deadlines and college-dormitory curfews, we now find ourselves confronted with babysitters' deadlines. On New Year's Eve I heard my husband plead with the sitter, "Couldn't we stay out past midnight tonight? All the other parents are doing it."

—MARGARET RALPH

✳ ✳ ✳ ✳ ✳ ✳ ✳ ✳ ✳ ✳ ✳ ✳

My daughter, her husband, and their three children planned to meet us at the Wilmington, Delaware, railroad station. My husband phoned and told them we were arriving on the 5:11 p.m. train. And, he added with a chuckle, "We want to be met by a brass band."

When we got off the train, we did not get our usual reception—no grandchildren came running to meet us. But as we approached the station, there stood our family, each one holding a musical instrument, one grandson conducting the band to the tune of "Seventy-six Trombones."

Passengers stood, smiling and laughing at the reception. The music, we discovered, was coming from a tape recorder—for not one of the family can play an instrument. Since it happened to be New Year's Eve, our family performance added a special aura of happiness to the train station.

—MRS. PHILIP GOODMAN

On Christmas Day all five of my sisters and their husbands were excitedly discussing their New Year's Eve plans. For the first time in many years, I was going to be alone that night, and anticipating that I might feel lonely, I asked one of my sisters if I could go to her house on New Year's.

"Of course you can!" she said enthusiastically.

And before I had a chance to thank her, she added, **"And if we're not home, the key will be above the door."**

—AUDRIE VANDER WERF

✳ ✳ ✳ ✳ ✳ ✳ ✳ ✳ ✳ ✳ ✳ ✳

My eldest daughter, Katherine, was home from college for the holidays and held a New Year's Eve party for her old high school friends. Billy arrived with all the makings of an Italian meal, which he had prepared in advance, including a large pot of sauce. The meal was a huge success.

A few days later, just before she returned to school, Katherine, her two younger sisters, and I went out for dinner.

"Oh," one of the girls said to Katherine in the car, "I forgot to tell you Billy called and left a message."

"What is it?"

"I can't tell you," she said. "Mom's here."

"Oh, come on," I protested. "Nothing can shock me."

"No way!" she said. "There's no way I'm repeating this."

After a lovely dinner, we returned home and the girls darted downstairs. A moment later Katherine came back up, laughing. "Do you know what Billy's message was? He said, 'Tell your sister I'm coming over to pick up my pot.' "

—WENDY STEWART

The party was getting under way, and our hostess, who had never before opened a bottle of champagne, was struggling with the cork. It popped out suddenly, dousing the gown of one guest.

The hostess was completely flustered until the soaking-wet woman saved the day by announcing gaily, **"At last I've been launched!"**

—MEGAN ADAMS

✳ ✳ ✳ ✳ ✳ ✳ ✳ ✳ ✳ ✳ ✳ ✳

Overheard: **"I have three trophies—two are for golf and one my wife gave me last New Year's day for watching only two out of three bowl games."**

—ANGIE PAPADAKIS

A snail made its way into a lounge one New Year's Eve and hopped up onto the bar. "What do you want?" the barman asked.

"I want a cocktail so I can celebrate with everyone else," the snail replied.

"I'm sorry, but we don't serve snails here. I'm going to have to ask you to leave."

"Only one drink, sir, and I'll be on my way," the snail pleaded.

"No. Furthermore, if you don't leave immediately, I'll be forced to evict you."

The snail persisted. "Just one—"

The barman, forming a circle with this thumb and finger, flicked the snail out the open window.

New Year's Eve arrived the next year, and the same barman was serving in the same lounge. To his surprise the same snail appeared on the bar. "What, you again? What do you want this time?" he shouted.

The snail replied, "What did you do that for?"

—BRAD GIESBRECHT

With a party going full bore in the apartment above his, my friend could forget about getting any sleep. The next day, he spotted the offending party giver.

"Didn't you hear me pounding on the ceiling?" he asked.

The woman smiled pleasantly. "That's okay. We were making a lot of noise ourselves."

—RALPH WARTH

QUOTABLE QUOTES

"The proper behavior all through the holiday season is to be drunk. This drunkenness culminates on New Year's Eve, when you get so drunk you kiss the person you're married to."

—P. J. O'ROURKE

"New Year's Day is every man's birthday."

—CHARLES LAMB

"Every new year is the direct descendant, isn't it, of a long line of proven criminals?"

—OGDEN NASH

"People are so worried about what they eat between Christmas and the New Year, but they really should be worried about what they eat between the New Year and Christmas."

—AUTHOR UNKNOWN

"May all your troubles last as long as your New Year's resolutions."

—JOEY ADAMS

"January is the month when we start paying on December bills and on November election results."

—JAMES HOLT MCGAVRAN

"Be always at war with your vices, at peace with your neighbors, and let each new year find you a better man."

—BENJAMIN FRANKLIN

"Youth is when you're allowed to stay up late on New Year's Eve. Middle age is when you're forced to."

—BILL VAUGHAN

✻ ✻ ✻ ✻ ✻ ✻ ✻ ✻ ✻ ✻ ✻ ✻

Starting on the Wrong Foot

Last New Year's Eve found me in the hospital scheduled for an operation to remove hemorrhoids. So while others donned party hats and sipped champagne, I wore a hospital gown and swigged painkillers.

That's not to say the holiday spirit was completely absent. The next day, January 1, I woke up to a banner on my bedroom wall.

It screamed: "Happy New Rear!"

—MARILYNN BELLMANN

Having just moved into a new neighborhood, I wanted to start out on the right foot and not disturb anybody with the New Year's Eve party I had planned. To test the sound from the television, I turned it on full blast, walked out of the house, closed the door, and listened. An awful amount of noise came through, and I tried to open the door to turn it off. But I was locked out. Since my wife would return soon, there was nothing to do but wait in the car, although I felt more like crawling under it.

Soon a neighbor came tearing out of his house and headed toward me. As he approached, he shouted above the racket, "Look, Mac, if you'd turn the damn thing down, you wouldn't have to sit out here to listen to it!"

—GROVER DUNN

George, an old friend, is an unusually calm, serene individual. One day he told me his secret. "Aunt Hildy," he said, "is an old lady in my town who is a great worrier. She fusses and frets over everything. So every New Year's Day I pay her a visit and hire her for one dollar a year to do all my worrying. She's an expert at it, and the price is right."

—FERN GREENWOOD

❄ ❄ ❄ ❄ ❄ ❄ ❄ ❄ ❄ ❄ ❄ ❄ ❄

My friend's parents run a big business and have little time for her. She always complains about that to me, and I always advise her to tell her parents how she feels. On New Year's Eve her parents asked what she wanted for New Year's.

My friend thought this was the perfect opportunity to talk with her parents. "I just want some time and warmth from you," she said.

As it turned out, her father gave her a watch, and her mother gave her a water heater.

—SIRIKANYA PHATHANAKUL

A drunk staggered into a bar shouting,
"Happy New Year, everybody!"
The fellow closest to him said,
"You turkey, it's the middle of May."
The bewildered drunk looked at him and cried,
"Oh, my gosh. My wife is going to kill me.
I've never been this late before."

—B. K.

After spending an excessive amount of money on Christmas, my husband decided to finish up the holiday week with one last grand flourish, and on New Year's Eve he gave me an exquisite white orchid. Attached was this card: Let the whiteness of this flower attest the purity of my love for you. Let the price of it measure in millions the joy you bring to me. Let the cellophane on the box represent the window of the poorhouse, where I'll soon be if this keeps up!

—BEATRICE J. STURM

✳ ✳ ✳ ✳ ✳ ✳ ✳ ✳ ✳ ✳ ✳ ✳

One New Year's Eve my wife and I decided to celebrate the advent of the new year in a rather sedate manner with two neighborhood couples. After a few rounds of bridge, a couple of highballs, and a midnight toast in champagne, however, I got a sudden urge to phone people in faraway places.

First, I called some good friends in Bermuda and wished them a Happy New Year. Then, feeling even more venturesome, I decided to call a first cousin in Germany, Dr. Hans Koehl. The operator told me that all circuits to Europe were busy, so I went to bed.

At 3:30 a.m. I was awakened by the message that the operator was still trying to put through my call. At that point, I was delighted. But at 6:30 a.m., when I wasn't feeling much like getting up, the phone rang again, with the news that the operator was ready with my call to Germany.

Reluctantly, in the freezing-cold bedroom and cold gray dawn, I said okay, whereupon I heard my cousin's voice saying in German: "Dr. Hans Koehl speaking. This is a recorded message. I will be away until Tuesday. In the meantime, please call my colleague, Dr. Max.

—ALBERT E. KOEHL

A professor was lecturing on the age of our planet and man's relatively recent appearance here. "If you were to telescope the entire history of the Earth into just a calendar year," he explained, "humans wouldn't show up until a few minutes before midnight on New Year's Eve." **"Hey,"** a student shouted, **"at least we made it for the party!"**

—CAROLYN VAN COTT

✳ ✳ ✳ ✳ ✳ ✳ ✳ ✳ ✳ ✳ ✳ ✳

Why didn't the calendar go to the New Year's party?

No one wanted to date it!

— ANONYMOUS

Driving home in thick traffic on New Year's Eve, our car dented the bumper of the vehicle ahead of us. As the driver started to get out of his car shouting at us, my friend who was driving our car leaned out and said with a smile, just helping you to start the new year with a bang.

The offended man accepted the apology, smiled, wishing us in return and drove off.

—N. MULLAN

My mother and sister were chatting on the telephone on New Year's Day but were persistently interrupted by crackling and other people's voices. "This line is terrible," remarked my mother.

"Yes," my sister agreed. "I'll call the telephone company to complain."

"There's no point. They won't be working today," said Mom.

"Yes, we are," interrupted a third voice. "We're trying to fix this crossed line."

—HUGH SLEIGHT

Some people's idea of celebrating the holidays is to have a Christmas they'll never forget and a New Year's Eve they can't remember.

—MAURICE SEITTER

✳ ✳ ✳ ✳ ✳ ✳ ✳ ✳ ✳ ✳ ✳ ✳

Weather reports from our previous hometown told of severe cold spells and heavy snows. Feeling a little smug over the warm, sunny climate we now live in, I couldn't resist sending a snapshot back to a good friend and former neighbor. It showed gay flowers blooming along a rustic fence and me in a light shirt and shorts, leaning casually against my lawn mower. On the back of the picture I wrote: "Taken on New Year's Day."

His reply arrived within the week—an indoor color shot of himself sitting by his fireplace, open book in lap, feet on a hassock, pipe in one hand, the other hand resting on the head of his big shepherd dog, who was lazily stretched beside the easy chair. The enclosed note read: "A darn shame you're still cutting grass in January."

—MARK HAYES

When my husband and I were teenagers, we went out on our first New Year's Eve date in the car he had recently bought. It was his first car, and he was enormously proud of it. At midnight, amid noisy horns and kissing, I waited eagerly for his romantic words. He looked into my eyes and said, **"Darn—my car is a year older now."**

—MARILYN MONDROSKI

✳ ✳ ✳ ✳ ✳ ✳ ✳ ✳ ✳ ✳ ✳ ✳

Hard-Working Holidays

My son's first job took him to Shenzhen, China. During the Chinese New Year, I asked Todd why it was called the Year of the Pig.

"I'm not sure," he wrote back. "A few months ago it was the Year of the Dog, and I'm still writing Dog on all my checks."

—PHAMA WOODYARD

During my years in Paris as a foreign correspondent, my wife and I came to expect a steady procession of visitors to our apartment the week between Christmas and New Year's. Every person who had served us in any way came then to ring the bell and hold out his palm for his "gift." There was the man who swept the gutter, the woman who sold flowers, the delivery boys, the postman, even the higher agent of the postes, who made a specialty of delivering nothing but registered letters. We doled out francs to them all.

One year, just when we thought there couldn't possibly be anyone else left to tip, the bell gave an imperious summons. I opened the door to a resplendent man in a tailcoat and a derby. I'd never laid eyes on him, and I thought he must be the chief assistant to the mayor of the arrondissement, at least. But no, he used the set formula: *"Bonjour, monsieur,* a happy New Year to you. A little present, if you please."

"Pardon me," I said, "but I can't remember ever having had the pleasure of seeing you."

"No," said the little man. "Monsieur has never viewed me, but I have served Monsieur and Madame and looked after their safety all through the long year. I, Monsieur," he said dramatically, "am the person who greases the elevator."

—BEN K. RALEIGH

✳ ✳ ✳ ✳ ✳ ✳ ✳ ✳ ✳ ✳ ✳ ✳ ✳

And then there was the psychiatrist who put a sign on his door that read: **"And a well-adjusted New Year to you all."**

—RUTH MACKAY

At a New Year's party of foreigners in Moscow, there was a champagne-fueled debate as to how the invisible Soviet agents manning the various "bugs" and tape recorders might be spending the holiday.

"Imagine the poor devils down at the KGB sitting around listening to all the parties tonight and not a drop to drink," said one Western diplomat, raising another glass.

A few minutes later the phone rang and the host answered. He heard no voice—only the unmistakable pop of a cork and the glug-glug pouring of champagne. Then the callers, anonymous as ever, hung up.

At the start of a new year, an employee came into the payroll office and asked, "Who do I talk to about changing my number of dependents?"

Before I could answer, my supervisor suggested, "How about your wife?"

—SANDRA L. GLAHN

At the army printing plant where I was assigned, much of the printed material was classified. All around the facility were reminders stressing the importance of maintaining secrecy. Visitors were given carefully supervised tours, and signs indicated areas that were off limits.

One day, just before Christmas, a beautiful banner was hung near the front entrance proclaiming, "Merry Christmas and Happy New Year." But after careful scrutiny, I noticed a hand-scrawled message below it: "To authorized personnel only."

—THOMAS J. VERBRUGGE

✳ ✳ ✳ ✳ ✳ ✳ ✳ ✳ ✳ ✳ ✳ ✳

Punts, Passes...

New Year's Day, and I had planned on spending it watching football. My wife, however, had other ideas, which resulted in my serving time at a family dinner. But when the coast was clear, I sneaked away and turned on the ball game. A few minutes later my wife came by with a cup of coffee for me.

"What's the score?" she asked.

"Zero-zero at the end of the third quarter," I told her.

"See?" she said, walking away. "You didn't miss a thing."

—HUY NGUYEN

It was the young bride's first New Year's Day in the married state. Her husband had spent all day sitting in front of the TV set, watching football games. The only time he said anything was when he demanded another beer.

At last she could bear it no longer. "I am going over to Mother's," she announced. "Maybe she will talk to me."

A shock awaited the bride, however. When she got to the home of her parents, her father was there alone, engrossed in the football games. Her mother was over at her mother's.

—ROBERT MCMORRIS

Not only did I have the usual Christmas and New Year's football games to contend with, but we had a new color television set as well. Finally, the Sunday after New Year's, I said in desperation to my husband, "Look, Bob, it's either me or this football game. Make your choice!"

He didn't take his eyes from the set. "Listen, Sal," he said. "Could we wait until half-time and see what we can salvage?"

—MRS. R. D. RUD

"I'm just picking up some New Year's Day football provisions."

✳ ✳ ✳ ✳ ✳ ✳ ✳ ✳ ✳ ✳ ✳ ✳

. . . and Promises

I made a resolution to start jogging again and needed to replace my running shoes. My sister Rebecca found a great deal on an expensive pair of shoes and bought them for me.

Later my boyfriend, Kyle, decided to come over and lend his support by jogging with me. So I put on my new shoes, and we went out. But I started to feel self-conscious, as he kept looking sideways at me.

Finally I stopped and said, "Okay, I know I don't run as much as you, but I'm trying my best here. So could you please stop staring at me like that?"

"Oh, that's not it at all, honey," Kyle said. "I'm just trying to figure out why you're jogging in cleats."

—SAMANTHA TOMICKI

On my list of New Year's resolutions was: "Be more patient with my daughter, Janet. No matter how irritating she is, remember that, after all, she is only 15 and is going through the exasperating period of adolescence."

Imagine then my feeling when, quite by accident, I came across Janet's New Year's resolutions and saw at the head of her list: "Try and be more patient with mother."

—MRS. C. R. KNOWLES

Last year when I called my parents to wish them a happy New Year, my dad answered the phone. "Well, Dad, what's your New Year's resolution?" I asked him.

"To make your mother as happy as I can all year," he answered proudly.

Then Mom got on, and I said, "What's your resolution, Mom?"

"To see that your dad keeps his New Year's resolution."

—JEANETTE CASE

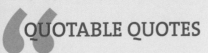

QUOTABLE QUOTES

"He who breaks a
resolution is a weakling;
He who makes one is a fool."

—F. M. KNOWLES

"Good resolutions
are simply checks
that men draw on
a bank where they
have no account."

—OSCAR WILDE

"A New Year's resolution is
something that goes in one year
and out the other."

—UNKNOWN

"New Year's Day now is the accepted time to
make your regular annual good resolutions.
Next week you can begin paving hell
with them as usual."

—MARK TWAIN

"Never tell your resolution beforehand,
or it's twice as onerous a duty."

—JOHN SELDEN

"New Year's Resolution:
To tolerate fools more
gladly, provided this does
not encourage them to take
up more of my time."

—JAMES AGATE

"Now there are more
overweight people
in America than
average-weight people.
So overweight people
are now average . . .
which means you have
met your New Year's
resolution."

—JAY LENO

"One swallow doesn't make a summer, but it
sure breaks a New Year's resolution."

—WILL ROGERS, JR.

"Would you like me to make a list of New Year's resolutions for you?"

✳ ✳ ✳ ✳ ✳ ✳ ✳ ✳ ✳ ✳ ✳ ✳

Some of those New Year's Eve hangovers last longer than some of those New Year's Eve resolutions.

—EARL WILSON

Hoping to excite student interest in our reading center, I asked each teacher to write a New Year's resolution on a special form and send it to me. After I posted the resolutions on the bulletin board in the reading center, one young teacher stopped by, looked at them for a few minutes, then left abruptly.

Passing two other teachers on their way in, she stormed, "My resolution isn't posted—and mine was one of the first ones in!"

I couldn't help but overhear, and the tone of her voice sent me flying to my desk in search of a misplaced resolution. Looking rapidly through stacks of papers, I uncovered hers. It read: "I resolve not to let little things upset me."

—JACKIE DAY

The trouble with making too many New Year's resolutions is that, if you stick to them, you could become impossible to live with.

—TONY ZARRO

Overheard: "Last year my New Year's resolutions were to lose weight, stop smoking, and marry Winona Ryder. **My only progress was sitting through *Little Women* without eating or lighting up.**"

—TONY PEYSER

Seasonal Silliness

"Once again, we come to the holiday season, a deeply religious time that each of us observes, in his own way, by going to the mall of his choice."

—DAVE BARRY

❄ ❄ ❄ ❄ ❄ ❄ ❄ ❄ ❄ ❄ ❄ ❄ ❄ ❄ ❄

That's Snow Funny!

Snow was falling heavily the day I decided to visit a car dealership. I was confident I'd get a great deal, figuring the salesmen would be desperate for customers on such a lousy day.

Sure enough, when I entered the showroom, I was the only client.

But my hope of getting a good deal quickly faded with the salesman's first words. "Boy," he said jovially, "you must want a new car real bad to come out on a day like this."

—TOM CARTER

My husband and I are from the "Live Free or Die" state, New Hampshire. Once, while visiting an island in the Caribbean, we started chatting with a resident, and our home state came up.

"I spent the coldest winter of my life in New Hampshire," he told us. "Your state motto really fits—'Live, Freeze and Die.' "

—CHRISTINA MCCARTHY

Returning to the University of Notre Dame after winter break one year, I was greeted by a freshly snow-blanketed campus. While admiring the scenery, a strange figure looming in the shadow of a campus building caught my eye. Directly under the words "Radiation Laboratory" on the side of the edifice stood a perfectly sculpted two-headed snowman.

—JESSICA WARD

During a storm, my wife's car became stuck in a snowbank. Our obstetrician saw her spinning her wheels, trying to get out. When he offered to help, my wife could not resist telling him, "Okay, Doctor. Now, when I count to three, push!"

—H. STEINBERG

"So much for the lemon. Let's try a carrot."

❄ ❄ ❄ ❄ ❄ ❄ ❄ ❄ ❄ ❄ ❄ ❄ ❄ ❄ ❄

Skiing is best when you have lots of white snow and plenty of Blue Cross.

—EARL WILSON

One October my wife and I spent a vacation on Washington's Olympic Peninsula. We were eager to visit the rain forests near the coast, but we heard that snowslides had made some of the roads impassable. Although apprehensive about the conditions we might run into, we drove on.

Sure enough, we had gone only a short way up the Hoh Rain Forest road when we saw a sign: "Ice 10 miles."

Five miles farther on, there was another: "Ice 5 miles."

The next one was: "Ice 1/2 mile."

We crept that half mile, then came to the last sign. It was outside a small grocery, and it read: "Ice 50¢."

—GIFFORD S. WALKER

Friends of ours, Sam and Ruth, from Maine had just bought a car when winter hit with all its fury. "I wonder if the car has seat warmers," Ruth wondered.

"It does," said Sam, looking through the owner's manual. "Here it is: rear defrosters."

—DALE DUTTON

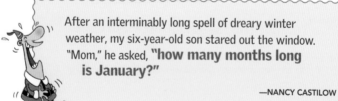

After an interminably long spell of dreary winter weather, my six-year-old son stared out the window. "Mom," he asked, **"how many months long is January?"**

—NANCY CASTILOW

 # QUOTABLE QUOTES

"I grew up thinking of snow as a luxury you visit."

—JOHN LANDIS

"To appreciate the beauty of a snowflake, it is necessary to stand out in the cold."

—UNKNOWN

"Each snowflake in an avalanche pleads not guilty."

—STANISLAW J. LEC

"When it snows, you have two choices: shovel or make snow angels."

—ANONYMOUS

"Getting an inch of snow is like winning 10 cents in the lottery."

—BILL WATTERSON

"Snow and adolescence are the only problems that disappear if you ignore them long enough."

—EARL WILSON

"Kindness is like snow— it beautifies everything it covers."

—ANONYMOUS

"Snowmen fall from heaven . . . unassembled."

—UNKNOWN

"A lot of people like snow. I find it to be an unnecessary freezing of water."

—CARL REINER

❄ ❄ ❄ ❄ ❄ ❄ ❄ ❄ ❄ ❄ ❄ ❄ ❄ ❄ ❄

Just getting out of the driveway was a major feat during last year's snow and ice storms. One coworker was relating how he used his seven-year-old son's baseball bat to smash the slick coat of ice on his driveway. He got cold and went inside for a cup of coffee before attempting to clear the car. Several minutes later his son, who had been outside with him, came in.

"Dad," he said, "I got the ice off the car."

"How did you do that?" his father asked.

"Same way you did," the boy shrugged, "with the baseball bat."

—JANINE JAQUET BIDEN

While traveling through Wyoming one winter day, I was experiencing what's called a horizontal blizzard. The snow that had fallen the day before was blowing across the road.

When I stopped for fuel, I remarked on the condition to a man at the gas station. He was obviously a local who had seen a lot of winters.

"Yeah," he said, nodding. "We don't get much snow, but what we do get, we use a lot."

—R. WAY

After I had attended a weeklong business meeting in sunny Orlando, Florida, my return flight to Philadelphia was canceled because of yet another snowstorm. My wife was not sympathetic when I called to report that I was spending another night in Orlando.

Arriving home the next day, I was greeted by a large sign on our garage door: "Dear 'Stranded in Orlando,' welcome to reality." Next to the sign was our snow shovel with a smaller sign attached. It read: "Reality."

—J. ROBERT BANKS

❄ ❄ ❄ ❄ ❄ ❄ ❄ ❄ ❄ ❄ ❄ ❄ ❄ ❄ ❄

Did you hear about the guy who froze to death at the drive-in? **He went to see "Closed for the Winter."**

—UNKNOWN

For several days mother had noticed a bulky parcel among the neat packages in our new quick-freeze chest but had been too busy to investigate. When she finally unwrapped it, she was amazed to find three dozen carefully shaped snowballs.

Inquiry about them was greeted by a wail from seven-year-old Billy. "Oh, Mother! Please don't throw them out! I'm going to make a lot of money selling genuine January snowballs on the Fourth of July."

—ELINOR M. CURD

Louie and his wife are listening to the radio when they hear the weather report: "A snow emergency has been declared. You must park your cars on the odd-numbered side of the street." So Louie gets up and moves his car.

Two days later, same thing. "A snow emergency has been declared," blares the radio. "Park your cars on the even-numbered side of the street." Louie gets up and does what he's told.

Three days later: "There will be a foot of snow today. Park your cars on the—" and then the power goes out.

"What should I do?" a confused Louie asks his wife.

"This time," she says, "why don't you just leave the car in the garage?"

—UNKNOWN

How do snowmen travel?
By icicle

Festive Follies

Late shoppers were frantically completing their Christmas purchases. The streets were filled with cars, and the sidewalks had barely enough room for shoppers. At one corner a middle-aged couple stood waiting for the light to change. The husband was so loaded down with packages that he could hardly see where he was going.

"Get back on the curb, George," his wife told him as he inched his way out into the street. But he paid no attention. Finally, in a voice that carried above the street noise, she said, "Well, if you're going to stand out there, let me carry the packages."

—THOMAS ARKWRIGHT

My six-year-old niece, Diana, often picks up minor illnesses in nursery school which means she has to stay at home for one or two weeks. So that she wouldn't be ill over Christmas, her parents didn't send her to nursery school from the middle of December

One day while out shopping, a kind acquaintance addressed her: "Why aren't you in nursery school, Diana. I hope there's nothing wrong," she said.

"No, nothing," was the reply. "I can't go, because I'm healthy."

—MARIANN SZAMOSI

Two kids are on their way to Sunday school when one says to the other, "What do you think about this Satan stuff?"

"Well, you remember Santa? This could turn out to be your Dad, too."

—PAT RUZSBATZKY

"It's very nice, but I asked for *boughs* of holly."

❄ ❄ ❄ ❄ ❄ ❄ ❄ ❄ ❄ ❄ ❄ ❄ ❄ ❄ ❄

Sign in a weight-loss center: **"24 shaping days until Christmas."**

—MRS. C. M. SWENSON

My grandmother has lived all her 80 years in northern New England, where what she sees from November until April is mostly snow. When my husband and I moved to California in January, we couldn't wait to phone and tell her about our green lawns, green trees, and flowers that bloom all winter long. "It sounds lovely, dear," she replied. "But doesn't it look terribly artificial?"

—MARGARET HEAGY

One of the rural community's biggest social events of the year was the Christmas program at the school, and my first-grade grandson was very excited about "speaking a piece" for this great affair. School was dismissed early that eagerly awaited day so everyone could be rested for the evening's events.

When Buster arrived home, he noticed that his sister had her hair up, his mother was pressing his dad's suit, etc. "Where are you all going?" he asked, concerned.

"To your Christmas program, dear," replied his mother. "Didn't you think we were going?"

"Well, I didn't think you'd have to come to the schoolhouse," he said. "I thought you'd be watching it on TV."

—MRS. WILLMA M. VEUM

I was recently talking with a friend who bemoaned her family's lack of holiday rituals. "My family doesn't have any traditions," she complained. "We just do the same thing year after year after year."

—NATALIE EDGE

To help our four-year-old son Eric learn to ski, I bought a harness that allows him to ski slowly on a leash. After a few practice runs on the rope tow, he and his father rode up the gondola with two experienced skiers.

"You must be a good little skier," one said to Eric.

"Yes," he said, "but I have to drag Dad along."

—VIRGINIA VICKERS BRAUN

A small boy in kindergarten was assigned by his teacher to make a Christmas drawing of the three Wise Men riding their camels across the desert. When the drawing was finished, the youngster took it to the teacher for her approval. She studied it and then pointed to an item—a square box with a couple of wires sticking out of it—that was being carried by one of the men.

"What's that?" she asked.

"Oh, that," said the boy. "That's the portable TV set. I didn't want them to miss *Gunsmoke!*"

—DAN BENNETT

My mother is a cleaning fanatic. One Saturday she told my brother and me to get down to the playroom and straighten it up. We had had a party there the previous evening, and she was none too happy about the mess.

As she watched us work, it was clear Mom was completely dissatisfied with our cleaning efforts and let us know it.

Finally my brother, exasperated with having to do it all over, reached for a broom and asked, "Can I use this, or are you planning to go somewhere?"

—MARK BERMAN

❄ ❄ ❄ ❄ ❄ ❄ ❄ ❄ ❄ ❄ ❄ ❄ ❄ ❄ ❄

The road by my house was in bad condition after a rough winter. Every day, I dodged potholes on the way to work. So I was relieved to see a construction crew working on the road one morning.

Later, on my way home, I noticed no improvement. But where the construction crew had been working stood a new, bright yellow sign with the words "Rough Road."

—SARAH KRAYBILL

Heavy snow had buried my van in our driveway.
My husband, Scott, dug around the wheels, rocked the van back and forth, and finally pushed me free. I was on the road when I heard an odd noise. I got on my cell and called home.
"Thank God you answered," I said when Scott picked up.
"There's this alarming sound coming from under the van.
For a moment I thought I was dragging you
down the highway."

"And you didn't stop?"

—PAIGE FAIRFIELD

Our minister was discussing various holidays and traditions with a flock of his young parishioners. "At Christmas," he said, "we traditionally use a plant called the poinsettia for decorating and giving, symbolizing Christmas. Can anyone tell me what plant we use to symbolize Easter?"

A hand shot up, and a small boy piped earnestly, "An eggplant?"

—GAIL P. HURST

❅ ❅ ❅ ❅ ❅ ❅ ❅ ❅ ❅ ❅ ❅ ❅ ❅ ❅ ❅

Sign posted in office: **"This year's Christmas party has been canceled due to last year's Christmas party."**

—ROBERT SYLVESTER

Over the years, I've tried to thank Mom for all her support throughout my college days at Illinois Wesleyan University. A chance to repay her came last winter. During her Christmas break from Depauw University in Indiana, where she is a fraternity housemother, Mom came to visit me in Florida. The morning after her arrival, I was late opening my art shop. The student waiting to buy supplies looked confused when I apologized and explained that my mother was home from college and I had been doing her laundry.

—BARBARA KLEIN CRAIG

My frugal aunt believes in buying paper napkins on sale, no matter what is printed on them. Thus, our family has become used to seeing Santa's face at Easter and wedding bells at Thanksgiving. But at one family reunion this practice puzzled a new in-law.

"Congratulations," he read on his napkin. "Congratulations for what?"

"Congratulations," my aunt said tersely. "You got a napkin!"

—F. R. KRANS

My son, Brian, was a theater major at Shenandoah University in Winchester, Virginia. He got a part in a local production and the director was telling the cast they would be doing a holiday musical called Yes, Virginia, There is a Santa Claus.

"Are you familiar with it?" he asked the cast members.

"Not really," Brian answered, completely serious. "I'm from New Jersey."

—NANCY CURL

❄ ❄ ❄ ❄ ❄ ❄ ❄ ❄ ❄ ❄ ❄ ❄ ❄ ❄ ❄

Sign in a men's clothing store: **"Make him feel like an astronaut—buy him long underwear for Christmas!"**

—IRVING KUPCINET

During the holiday season, my husband, Gordon, called one day to say we had been invited to a party that night at a client's house. A little later he phoned back. "Honey, I'm going to have to meet you at the party. I'm running late."

"But I don't know these people," I protested.

"Just tell them you're Gordon's wife."

It was snowing heavily, and many street signs were covered. But I eventually found the street and spotted cars and a party in full swing.

I was greeted warmly at the door, plied with food and beverage, and met everyone. After some time I went to the host and asked him if he'd heard from Gordon.

"Gordon? Who's Gordon?"

My heart sank. "You're not Reed, are you?

"No," he laughed. "He lives five houses down."

—DENISE LEAVITT

With the Christmas season over, two ministers in our town began teasing a third because the stable for a nativity scene was still standing on the lawn at his church. The figures had been removed, but the wooden shed and bales of straw remained. Toward the end of January, with the stable still there, the two ministers decided to act. On the empty stall they placed a large sign proclaiming: **"Gone to Egypt."**

—MRS. EDWARD R. JAEGER

❄ ❄ ❄ ❄ ❄ ❄ ❄ ❄ ❄ ❄ ❄ ❄ ❄ ❄ ❄

As I was leaving a formal dinner party in the early hours of the morning, I remembered that the motor of my new Mercedes-Benz had been hotter than it should have been. Realizing that I might not find a service station open, I asked my host for a bucket of water. No bucket was available, but my resourceful host handed me a large paper sack containing three champagne magnums filled with water. Once on the street, I felt rather ridiculous as, dressed in my tuxedo, I proceeded to empty the water into the radiator. Then two passers-by stopped in amazement, and one said to the other, "These Mercedes owners really do pamper their cars, don't they?"

—Y. YOGASUNDRAM

For years my mother and aunt had exchanged ten-dollar bills at Christmas. When they both became widows, they reduced the exchange to five dollars. This year, to cut expenses even more, they decided not to exchange gifts at all!

—JACK I. KIBBEN

To add a personal touch to his Christmas cards, a friend of ours decided to have the local ones delivered by hand. He told his son he would get two cents for each card delivered. Later the boy returned. "Some people said they had enough Christmas cards," he said. "Others paid the two cents, and Mr. Jones only had a nickel."

—CINDA WARNER

I asked my mother-in-law if she enjoyed the flight back from her vacation.

"Yes," she said, "but we had to keep our seat belts on because of all the flatulence."

—MERVYN SAUNDERS

"Room 721, sir. Ah, yes ... the Nutcracker Suite!"

❄ ❄ ❄ ❄ ❄ ❄ ❄ ❄ ❄ ❄ ❄ ❄ ❄ ❄ ❄

People sometimes have trouble believing that the name of our town is George. Last New Year's Day, for example, my brother, about 150 miles away in Seattle, telephoned us. We had just begun our conversation when we were cut off.

My brother immediately dialed the long-distance operator and pleaded, "Operator, I was talking to George, Washington, and you cut us off."

Apparently, she thought someone was still celebrating, for she replied, "Anyone who's been gone that long, we only allow thirty seconds."

—MRS. AUBREY STRONG

I was shopping in a large department store in mid-January. All the rush of the holiday and post-holiday sales was over, and the place seemed quite empty. One saleswoman, however, was swamped in packages. As she went by me with an armload of boxes, she explained, "MacArthurs."

A few minutes later she passed me again with another batch of cartons. "More MacArthurs," she said. Then I saw her again— and again—with still more packages. "Full of MacArthurs," she said, smiling.

When I saw her for the fifth time, I asked, "Miss, could you tell me what in the world MacArthurs are?" As she carried away yet another armload, she winked at me and said, "I shall return."

—RENNY HARTMANN

Why are there only snowmen and no snowwomen?

Because only men are crazy enough to stand out in the snow all winter.

❄❄❄❄❄❄❄❄❄❄❄❄❄❄

Sign on a St. Louis church bulletin board:
**"Merry Christmas to our Christian friends.
Happy Hanukkah to our Jewish friends.
And to our atheist friends, good luck."**

—WILLIAM E. BURKE

At our traditional Christmas family gathering, relatives who hadn't seen one another for a year were catching up on news. One loud voice above the babble commented, "Looks like you've put on a little weight."

The remark was addressed to my youngest son. However, all conversation in the room stopped as everyone responded, "Oh, maybe a couple of pounds."

—PAT RICE

While shopping in a Bowling Green, Kentucky, drugstore one January day, I noticed an old man approach the counter, hat in hand, and ask the druggist for one of the store's free almanacs.

Receiving the almanac, he thanked the druggist and added, "I sure appreciate this. Last year I didn't get a copy and had to take the weather just as it came."

—W. E. FINCH

Ice-fisherman Floyd Colburn, of Grand Rapids, Michigan, got tired of catching and throwing back small perch. Finding a Christmas ribbon in his pocket, he began tying pretty red bows on each perch before throwing it back. It wasn't long before another fisherman came dashing up to him, wide-eyed, and cried, "You won't believe what I'm going to tell you!"

—JIM KIMBALL

❄ ❄ ❄ ❄ ❄ ❄ ❄ ❄ ❄ ❄ ❄ ❄ ❄ ❄ ❄

Last Christmas I put up colored lights in the form of the word PEACE on the side of the barn. The lights were still in place several weeks later, although we had not turned them on since New Year's.

One evening I turned into my drive and saw the word PEACE glowing on the barn. I wondered what the occasion could be, until I got out of my car and saw that my wife had put a fresh dent in the family station wagon.

—BERNARD J. WEISS

To entertain a business partner from England last winter, my father took him to a restaurant in Butte, Montana. They ordered red wine, which arrived icy cold, seemingly straight from the refrigerator.

"Oh, Miss," my father's guest said, gesturing to the waitress. "Red wine should be served at room temperature."

"Is that right?" she replied. "Then maybe you should come visit us again in July."

—RAMONA RADONICH

I was getting a little exasperated with my four-year-old daughter, Eloise, and her constant questions about Mary, Jesus, and the nativity story. **After explaining to her that I wasn't sure of Mary's exact features, Eloise suggested I add her as a Facebook friend to find out.**

—AMANDA WEBSTER

❄ ❄ ❄ ❄ ❄ ❄ ❄ ❄ ❄ ❄ ❄ ❄ ❄ ❄

Four-year-old, bursting into song:
"Hark! The hairy angels sing,"

—LIDA LARKIN

"Save during our January white sales," read a sign visible for blocks in Grosse Pointe, a wealthy suburb of Detroit. We drove up to the sign expecting to find the usual window display of linen but instead found Grosse Pointe's version of the white sales—an automobile showroom filled with white Cadillacs.

—MRS. PETER J. THOMAS

On a chilly winter evening, my husband and I were snuggled together on the floor watching television. During a commercial break, he reached over and gave my foot a gentle squeeze.

"Mmmm," I said. "That's sweet."

"Actually," he admitted, "I thought that was the remote."

—STEPHANIE EELE

As a financial-aid counselor at a state university, I work with many students. Recently a young woman named Noel came to my office. Thinking to put her at ease, I asked if she had been born around Christmas.

"No," she replied. "Actually, my birthday is September 25." Then her expression brightened, and she added, "But I suppose originally I was a Christmas present."

—MILFORD JOHNSON

What do you get when you cross a snowman with a vampire?

Frostbite

DUSTIN GODSEY

"Uh, oh. Gotto run, Dave. Here comes the ol' ball and hook."

When testing our hospital's pharmacy computer system, we chose names such as Bugs Bunny and Buffy the Vampire Slayer for our fictitious patients so there would be no mix-ups with real people. Just before Christmas, the test name Santa Claus was used. It wasn't long before a preoperative medication for Santa was returned to the pharmacy with the notation: "Operation on hold until he finishes work on December 25."

—HELENE LAU

Jokes Around the Table

Lost in the desert for three days, a man suddenly hears, "Mush!"

Looking up, he sees what he thinks is a mirage: an Eskimo on a sled, driving a team of huskies. To his surprise, the sled comes to a stop at his feet seconds later.

"I don't know why you're here, but thank goodness," the man says. "I've been lost for days."

Panting, the Eskimo replies, "You think *you're* lost?"

—ROBERT LUTZ

Although fighting the enemy is considered normal, the army frowns upon fighting among the troops. So much so that after one too many battles royal, my uncle was ordered to undergo a psychiatric evaluation in which he had to endure some odd questions.

"If you saw a submarine in the Sahara, what would you do?"

"Well, I'd throw snowballs at it," he answered.

"Where'd you get the snowballs?" the doctor asked.

"Same place you got the submarine."

—HANNAH ETCHISON

Longtime friends were celebrating their 50th anniversary. One of their sons gave a loving toast, finishing with, "And thank you for having such a beautiful marriage."

"Thank you for making it necessary," the father joked.

In the silence that followed, his wife whispered, **"Not him. He's the second son."**

—DOT WILSON

A man suffering from a miserable cold begs his doctor for relief. The doctor prescribes pills. But after a week, the man's still sick. So the doctor gives him an injection. But that doesn't help his condition either.

"OK, this is what I want you to do," says the doctor on the third visit. "Go home and take a hot bath. Then throw open all the windows and stand in the draft."

"I'll get pneumonia!" protests the patient.

"I know. That I can cure."

—UNKNOWN

❄❄❄❄❄❄❄❄❄❄❄❄❄❄❄

Fatherhood is pretending the present you love most is soap-on-a-rope.

—BILL COSBY

Late one foggy night, a Yankees fan and a Red Sox fan collide head-on while driving across a bridge. Fortunately, both are unhurt, but their cars are pretty banged up.

"This is a sign," says the Yankees fan, "that we should put away our differences and live as friends instead of rivals."

"You're right," says the Red Sox fan. He pops open the trunk and takes out a bottle of bourbon. "Let's toast our newfound friendship."

The Yankees fan takes a big swig and hands back the bottle. "Your turn!"

"Nah," says the Sox fan, tossing the bottle into the river. "I think I'll just wait for the police to show up."

—FRANK BACHARD

"Mom, is God the one who puts food on our table?"

"Yes, He is, my child."

"Is Santa Claus the one who brings us gifts at Christmas?"

"Of course."

"Did the stork bring me?"

"Yes, it did, sweetheart."

"Then what good is Daddy?"

—FABIANO SANTOS DUARTE

How do you fix a broken tomato?

A twelve-step program to keep it from getting sauced.

JIM RAU

When I tell people that I am an explosive ordinance disposal technician, I usually need to go into further detail about what I do. Once I was with my eight-year-old son when I was explaining my job to someone. "I defuse live bombs," I said.

"Yeah," my son added. **"If you see him running, you'd better catch up!"**

—THOMAS LIGON

"I was at a dinner party the other night, and one woman had on a dress that was cut so low, you had to look under the table to see what she was wearing."

—JOEY ADAMS

Eve, in the Garden of Eden, called out, "Lord, I have a problem."

And the Lord said, "What's the matter, Eve?"

"I know you created me and this beautiful garden. But I'm lonely—and I'm sick of eating apples."

"Well, in that case," replied the Almighty, "I'll create a man for you."

"What's a man?"

"He's a flawed creature with aggressive tendencies, an enormous ego, and an inability to listen. But he's big and fast and muscular. He'll be really good at fighting and kicking a ball and hunting animals—and not bad in the sack."

"Sounds great!" replied Eve.

"There's one condition," added the Lord. "You'll have to let him believe that I made him first."

—MONICA HYSON

"Oh sure!! Run away when there's work to do!"

❄ ❄ ❄ ❄ ❄ ❄ ❄ ❄ ❄ ❄ ❄ ❄ ❄ ❄ ❄

Spotted outside a church in Michigan:
**"Honk if you love Jesus. Keep on texting while
you drive if you want to meet Him."**

—GINA VESELY

I stopped by my church in time for Communion. As I left my pew to approach the altar, I spotted this sign on the wall: "Please don't leave your personal things unattended lest someone assume that these are the answers to their prayers."

—BIENVENIDO GONZALEZ

After reading up on the finer points of ice fishing, a young woman heads onto the ice. Just as she's about to drill her first hole, a booming voice from above bellows, "There are no fish under the ice!"

The woman is startled, but she keeps drilling.

Again the voice thunders, "There are no fish under the ice!"

Now the woman is shaking. But she takes a deep breath, and just as she's about to cut a new hole—

"There are no fish under the ice!"

The frightened woman looks skyward and asks, "Is that you, Lord?"

"No. This is the manager of the skating rink!"

—UNKNOWN

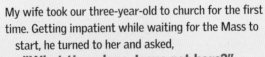

My wife took our three-year-old to church for the first time. Getting impatient while waiting for the Mass to start, he turned to her and asked,
"What time does Jesus get here?"

—UNKNOWN

✳ ✳ ✳ ✳ ✳ ✳ ✳ ✳ ✳ ✳ ✳ ✳ ✳ ✳ ✳

Head of household: **We jingle the bells in December and juggle the bills in January.**

—MARY H. WALDRIP

Visiting a village in a Third World nation, an American dignitary tells the local inhabitants, "I bring you warm greetings from my people!"

The locals respond, "Kazanga!"

"We wish you prosperity!"

"Kazanga!" they bellow.

"I promise years of friendship and economic benefit!"

"Kazanga! Kazanga!"

As the dignitary leaves the podium, he tells the chief, "That went well."

"Uh-huh," the chief replies, adding, "Look out! Don't step in the kazanga."

—UNKNOWN

I've never understood the concept of the gift certificate, because for the same 50 bucks, my friend could've gotten me 50 bucks.

—UNKNOWN

Ten men and one woman are hanging on to a rope that extends down from a helicopter. The weight of 11 people is too much for the rope, so the group decides one person has to jump off.

No one can decide who should go, until finally the woman volunteers. She gives a touching speech, saying she will sacrifice her life to save the others, because women are used to giving up things for their husbands and children.

When she finishes speaking, all the men start clapping.

—MARGARET PITMAN

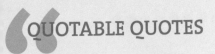

QUOTABLE QUOTES

"I once **wanted to become an atheist**, but I gave up—they have no holidays."

—HENNY YOUNGMAN

"I'm glad that life isn't like a Christmas song, because if my friends and I were building a snowman and it suddenly came alive when we put a hat on it, I'd probably freak and stab it to death with an icicle."

—MATTHEW PERRY

"**Happiness is having a large, loving, caring, close-knit family in another city.**"

—GEORGE BURNS

"Airport screeners are now scanning holiday fruitcakes. Not even the scanners can tell what those little red things are."

—DAVID LETTERMAN

"**A good holiday is one spent among people whose notions of time are vaguer than yours.**"

—J. B. PRIESTLEY

"**Nothing says holidays like a cheese log.**"

—ELLEN DEGENERES

"At this time of the year, with the holidays upon us, nothing says she cares about how I am, where I am and what I'm doing as much as the restraining order."

—RANDY SAINT

"**No self-respecting mother would run out of intimidations on the eve of a major holiday.**"

—ERMA BOMBECK

What sound does a grape make when an elephant steps on it?

None. It just lets out a little wine.

In the spring I planted a small vegetable garden and looked after it with great pride as it flourished. Then came the summer day when I said to myself, "The first thing in the morning, I'll harvest my crop."

But before I got outside, my small son dashed in, yelling, "Mama, the ducks are in our garden." What a feast my neighbor's fowl had! Not a bean vine was left standing. Squashed tomatoes were all over. I bawled. My neighbor apologized. Months later, after all was forgiven and forgotten, the neighbor came to wish us a merry Christmas. He handed me a package, which he said I must open right away.

We all burst into laughter when we saw the gift—a plump duck all ready to pop into the oven, with this note attached: "Enjoy your garden."

—MRS. PLEAS OVERBY

A Florida man protested a tax clerk's ruling that a baby born on January 24 was not deductible on last year's income. "Why not?" he asked. "It was last year's business!"

—DORA JANE DEMING

Mystery writer P. D. James told a college audience that her career path was laid out early in life. "My parents had an inkling of what I might become when I was five years old. When they read me 'Humpty Dumpty,' I asked, 'Was he pushed?'"

—SHIRLEY SAYRE

❄ ❄ ❄ ❄ ❄ ❄ ❄ ❄ ❄ ❄ ❄ ❄ ❄ ❄ ❄ ❄

A man walks up to an attractive girl in a disco and asks, "Would you like to dance?"

"I wouldn't dance with you if you were the last man on earth," she snorts.

"I don't think you heard me correctly," the man says. "I said, 'You look fat in those pants.'"

—SERRA ADALAR

A group of middle-aged people came into the roller-skating rink my wife and I own. One explained that none of them had skated in 15 years, but they thought it would be fun to give it a try. I had handed out eight pairs of skates before asking the last person in the group what size he needed.

"No, thanks," he said. "I'm the designated driver."

—MIKE WILLIAMS

Did you hear about the doctor who went on a ski trip and got lost on the slopes? He stamped out "help" in the snow, but nobody could read his writing.

—HAROLD ZUBER

My five-year-old son and I were discussing some of the differences between his childhood and mine. I pointed out that when I was young, we didn't have Nintendo, cell phones, computers, or even digital cameras.

I realized just how difficult this was for him to comprehend when he asked, **"Did you have fruit?"**

—MICHELLE PORTER

"Now, let me get this straight—four calling birds, three French hens, two turtle doves, *and* a partridge in a pear tree?!"

❄ ❄ ❄ ❄ ❄ ❄ ❄ ❄ ❄ ❄ ❄ ❄ ❄ ❄ ❄

Alice and Ted went snowboarding, and Ted brought along a quart-size thermos. Alice had never seen one and asked what it was. "It's a thermos," replied Ted. "The guy at the store told me it's used for keeping hot things hot and cold things cold."

"Sounds great," said Alice. "What do you have in it?"

"Three coffees and a Popsicle."

—JEANNE STANTON

My wife, a professor of medicine, has published five books. After she'd written her latest one, I stopped at a market to buy some chocolate and champagne.

"Are you celebrating something?" asked the clerk as he bagged my items.

"Yes," I replied proudly. "My wife just finished a book."

He paused a moment. "Slow reader?"

—DENNIS DOOK

A couple of fishing buddies from Alabama decided to travel to Minnesota one winter to try ice fishing. Just before they reached the frozen lake, they stopped at a bait shop to buy supplies. "Don't forget an ice pick," one of them said. They paid for their purchases and were off.

Two hours later, one of them returned. "We need another dozen ice picks," he said. He bought a whole box full and left. But in an hour, he was back.

The bait man asked, "How are you fellows doing?"

"Not too well," the fisherman replied. "We haven't even got the boat in the water yet."

—STANTON SEEPERSAUD

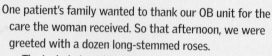

One patient's family wanted to thank our OB unit for the care the woman received. So that afternoon, we were greeted with a dozen long-stemmed roses.

The included card began,

"To the Obese staff . . ."

—SHEREE CHRISTENSEN

According to the order form, if I wanted a school photograph of my first-grader, there was one simple rule I had to adhere to: "Your child must be present at the time the picture is taken."

—LEAH BANG

I was looking at the pies offered by a nearby café. They had cherry, apple, berry, peach, and Herman's.

"What type of pie is Herman's?" I asked the waiter.

"Apple," he said.

"Then why is it called Herman's pie?"

"Because Herman called in to reserve it."

—MARY SKORDINSKY

Just before Christmas, we had as visitors two young couples from Hong Kong, where it never snows. I decided to drive them to a mountain ski area and let them have the experience of being in deep snow and of riding the ski lift.

As we drove up the canyon through the green pines with their sparkling white mantle, our visitors were wide-eyed with the beauty of it all. One man said quietly, "I feel as if I'm right inside my own Christmas card."

—T. FRANK NELSON

❄ ❄ ❄ ❄ ❄ ❄ ❄ ❄ ❄ ❄ ❄ ❄ ❄ ❄ ❄

Seen in the window of a camping shop:
"Now is the winter of our discount tents."

—PAMELA KILGOUR

When a woman in my office became engaged, a colleague offered her some advice. "The first ten years are the hardest," she said.

"How long have you been married?" I asked.

"Ten years," she replied.

—TONYA WINTER

I answer a lot of questions at the information desk at Olympic National Park, in Washington State. But one visitor stumped me: "Do you have any trails that just go downhill?"

—MIKE PERZEL

During our church service one Sunday, a parishioner was speaking about an emotionally charged topic and had trouble controlling her tears. Finishing her remarks, she told the congregation, "I apologize for crying so much. I'm usually not such a big boob."

The bishop rose to close the session and remarked, "That's okay. We like big boobs."

—L.S.

The highlight of our zoo trip was a peacock showing off its plumage. My four-year-old son was particularly taken with it. That evening, he couldn't wait to tell his father: "Dad, guess what! I saw a Christmas tree come out of a chicken!"

—CAROL HOWARD

America's Funniest Jokes, Quotes, and Cartoons from Reader's Digest

Laughter, the Best Medicine

More than 600 jokes, gags, and laugh lines. Drawn from one of the most popular features of *Reader's Digest* magazine, this lighthearted collection of jokes, one-liners, and other glimpses of life is just what the doctor ordered.

ISBN 978-0-89577-977-9 • $9.95 paperback

Laughter Really Is the Best Medicine

Guaranteed to put laughter in your day, this sidesplitting compilation of jokes and lighthearted glimpses of life is drawn from *Reader's Digest* magazine's most popular humor column. Poking fun at the facts and foibles of daily routines, this little volume is sure to tickle your funny bone.

ISBN 978-1-60652-204-2 • $9.95 paperback

Laughter, the Best Medicine @ Work

A laugh-out-loud collection of jokes, quotes, and quips designed to poke fun at the workplace. Laugh your way through the 9-to-5 grind with this mix of hilarious wisecracks, uproarious one-liners, and outrageous résumés. No matter how bad your day, you'll find that laughter really *is* the best medicine for all your work woes.

ISBN 978-1-60652-479-4 • $9.99 paperback

Laughter, the Best Medicine: Those Lovable Pets

People are funny, but so are the animals we love, and this book brings to life the often entertaining relationships we have with our animals. A chuckle-inducing collection dedicated to the companions we hold so dear—our pets.

ISBN 978-1-60652-357-5 • $9.99 paperback

For more information, visit us at RDTradePublishing.com
E-book editions are also available.

Reader's Digest books can be purchased through retail and online bookstores.
In the United States books are distributed by Penguin Group (USA) Inc.
For more information or to order books, call 1-800-788-6262.